Extending
the
Challenge
in Mathematics

To Dan, Chris, Tyler, and all the other promising young mathematicians
who shared their mathematical creations with me.
Thanks for the inspiration.

Extending the Challenge
in Mathematics

Developing Mathematical Promise
in K-8 Students

Linda Jensen Sheffield

CORWIN PRESS, INC
A Sage Publications Company
2455 Teller Road
Thousand Oaks, CA 91320-2218

Call: (800) 818-7243   Fax: (800) 417-2466
www.corwinpress.com

For information:

Corwin Press, Inc.
A Sage Publications Company
2455 Teller Road
Thousand Oaks, California 91320
www.corwinpress.com

Sage Publications Ltd.
6 Bonhill Street
London EC2A 4PU
United Kingdom

Sage Publications India Pvt. Ltd.
M-32 Market
Greater Kailash I
New Delhi 110 048 India

Printed in the United States of America

Library of Congress Cataloging-in-Publication Data

Sheffield, Linda Jensen, 1949–
Extending the challenge in mathematics: Developing mathematical promise in K-8 students / by Linda Jensen Sheffield.
    p. cm.
"In Association with the Texas Association for the Gifted and Talented."
Includes bibliographical references and index.
ISBN 0-7619-3850-8 (cloth)
ISBN 0-7619-3851-6 (paper)
1. Mathematics-Study and teaching-United States. 2. Gifted children-Education-United States. I. Title.
QA13 .S49 2003
372.7'0973-dc21   2002013710

This book is printed on acid-free paper.

02 03 04 05 10 9 8 7 6 5 4 3 2 1

Acquisitions Editor:	Kylee Liegl
Copy Editor:	Barbara Coster
Production Editor:	Denise Santoyo
Typesetter:	Tina Hill
Indexer:	Molly Hall
Cover Designer:	Tracy E. Miller
Production Artist:	Sandy Ng

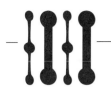

Contents

Reproducible Forms

4. Geometry and Measurement

5. Data Analysis and Probability

About the Author

Linda Sheffield is Regents Professor of Mathematics Education at Northern Kentucky University. She directs the graduate program for teachers of the gifted at Northern Kentucky University and has conducted several grant-funded programs designed to encourage teachers and students in the areas of mathematics and science. She has written numerous books and articles for both teachers and students and has conducted seminars for teachers across the United States and as far away as Spain, Germany, England, Sicily, Japan, Australia, China, and Hungary. Her books include PreK–2 NCTM Navigations series, a series of math problem-solving books for children in third through eighth grade, an integrated math/science book for teachers of preschool through primary school children, and a math methods book for elementary and middle school teachers. She is past president of the School Science and Mathematics Association (SSMA) and was chair of the Task Force on Promising Students for the National Council of Teachers of Mathematics (NCTM). She was also editor of the NCTM book *Developing Mathematically Promising Students*. She received her M.Ed. and Ph.D. in Mathematics Education from the University of Texas at Austin and her bachelor's degree from Iowa State University.

CORWIN
PRESS

The Corwin Press logo—a raven striding across an open book—represents the happy union of courage and learning. We are a professional-level publisher of books and journals for K-12 educators, and we are committed to creating and providing resources that embody these qualities. Corwin's motto is "Success for All Learners."

Developing Mathematical Promise 1

The student most neglected, in terms of realizing full potential, is the gifted student of mathematics. Outstanding mathematical ability is a precious societal resource, sorely needed to maintain leadership in a technological world.

NCTM (1980), *An Agenda for Action: Recommendations for School Mathematics of the 1980s* (p. 18)

This need to nurture outstanding mathematical ability is even more critical today than it was over 20 years ago when the National Council of Teachers of Mathematics (NCTM) cited this necessity in their *Agenda for Action* for the 1980s. Today we realize that mathematical ability is not something that students are born with that will develop on its own. The development of mathematical potential, like any other valued ability, is something that takes dedication and hard work on the part of teachers, parents, and the students themselves. One of the goals of this book is to give teachers one more resource to help students develop their mathematical promise.

WHAT IS MATHEMATICAL PROMISE?

In 1995, the NCTM appointed a Task Force on Mathematically Promising Students charged with rethinking the traditional definition of mathematically gifted students to broaden it to the more inclusive idea of mathematically promising students. In the *Report of the NCTM Task Force on Mathematically Promising Students* (Sheffield, Bennett, Beriozábal, DeArmond, & Wertheimer, 1995),

Some of the material in this chapter is adapted from Sheffield, Linda. (February 2000). Creating and Developing Promising Young Mathematicians. *Teaching Children Mathematics, 6*(6), 416-419, 426. Copyright © 2000 by the National Council of Teachers of Mathematics. Used with permission.

2   EXTENDING THE
CHALLENGE IN   — !!!
MATHEMATICS

mathematically promising students are defined as those who have the potential to become the leaders and problem solvers of the future. The intent was to go beyond the concept of mathematically gifted students, who traditionally had been defined as the top 3 to 5% of students based upon some standardized mathematics test. This outdated notion of mathematical giftedness frequently unnecessarily restricts access to interesting, challenging mathematics to a very small portion of the population.

The NCTM Task Force defined mathematically promising students as a function of variables that ought to be maximized. In the *Report of the NCTM Task Force*, mathematical promise is described as a function of the following:

- Ability
- Motivation
- Belief
- Experience or opportunity

The Task Force acknowledged that these variables were ones that could and should be developed in all students if we are going to maximize the numbers and levels of students with mathematical talent. This description recognizes that mathematical abilities can be enhanced and developed and are not something that some portion of the population is lacking due to some genetic deficiency. It acknowledges recent brain-functioning research that documents changes in the brain due to experiences. We know that the brain grows and develops as it responds to challenging problems, and mathematics is the perfect venue for this development

This definition also concedes that students are not always motivated to achieve at their highest possible levels, and that the popular culture in the United States may even encourage students to disguise their mathematical abilities in order to avoid negative labels such as "nerd" or "geek." Belief in one's ability to succeed and belief in the importance of mathematical success by the students themselves, teachers, peers, and parents are also recognized as important; lack of such beliefs, especially by females, students of color, students from lower socioeconomic groups, and students for whom English is a second language, are acknowledged as a significant barrier to learning for a large number of students.

The importance of the fourth variable, experience or opportunity to learn, is especially evident when one notes the disparity in mathematics course offerings in middle schools and high schools across the United States. In many U.S. high schools, students do not have any access to challenging mathematics courses such as Advanced Placement calculus or statistics, or if these courses are available, they are only available to a small percentage of the students in the school. This is in sharp contrast to countries such as Japan, where all students are expected to master the basics of calculus along with other topics such as discrete mathematics, probability, statistics, geometry, and number theory in a challenging, integrated high school mathematics curriculum.

WHO ARE MATHEMATICALLY PROMISING?

If we are to be successful in developing ever-increasing numbers of mathematically promising students, we need to be aware of some of the characteristics that these students demonstrate. Many researchers have noted that students with mathematical talent often display a mathematical frame of mind, they are able to think logically and construct generalizations, and they exhibit mathematical creativity, curiosity, and perseverance. The following list includes a few of the specific characteristics that we might look for and nurture in a mathematically promising student. Please note that not all promising students will exhibit all or even most of these characteristics. These are indicators of potential mathematically promising talent that should be developed as much as possible in all students. Teachers and parents should strive to find interesting mathematical challenges at all levels that will engage students in this development of mathematical power.

CHARACTERISTICS OF A MATHEMATICALLY PROMISING STUDENT

MATHEMATICAL FRAME OF MIND

1. Loves exploring patterns and puzzles
2. Sees mathematics and structure in a variety of situations
3. Recognizes, creates, and extends patterns
4. Organizes and categorizes information
5. Has a deep understanding of simple mathematical concepts, including a strong number sense

MATHEMATICAL FORMALIZATION AND GENERALIZATION

1. Generalizes the structure of a problem, often from only a few examples
2. Uses proportional reasoning
3. Thinks logically and symbolically with quantitative and spatial relations
4. Develops proofs and other convincing arguments

MATHEMATICAL CREATIVITY

1. Processes information flexibly—switches from computation to visual to symbolic to graphic representations as appropriate in solving problems
2. Reverses processes—can switch from a direct to a reverse train of thought
3. Has original approaches to problem solving—solves problems in unique ways, tries unusual methods
4. Strives for mathematical elegance and clarity in explaining reasoning

MATHEMATICAL CURIOSITY AND PERSEVERANCE

1. Is curious about mathematical connections and relationships—asks "why" and "what if"
2. Has energy and persistence in solving difficult problems
3. Digs beyond the surface of a problem, continues to explore after the initial problem has been solved

The following characteristics may be useful in a mathematics class but are not necessary for a student to be mathematically promising:

1. Speed and accuracy with computation
2. Memory for formulas and facts
3. Spatial ability

Sheffield, Fall 2000, pp. 7–8. Used with permission of the Kentucky Association for Gifted Education.

In this book, you will find numerous examples of problems and questions designed to encourage and enhance students' mathematical promise. It is hoped that together with the students, you will create many other intriguing problems and puzzles for yourselves.

WHAT ARE THE GOALS OF MATHEMATICS INSTRUCTION?

Suggestions for ways in which teachers, parents, and students can work together to increase levels of mathematical power and proficiency are given throughout this book. The intent is to move students along a continuum such as the following:

innumerates   doers   computers   consumers   problem   problem   creators
                                                   solvers   posers

This model notes that some students are virtually innumerate, lacking even basic concepts of number and computation. Slightly above these are students who can do some mathematics or who are good at basic computation, but who do not apply these concepts to everyday problems. Students who are wise consumers are better able to function in our increasingly technological world, but this is not sufficient. In the 1980 NCTM *Agenda for Action*, problem solving was noted as a major goal for the end of the 20th century. However, even this is not enough for the problems that we face in the 21st century. Students today must be able to not only solve the problems that others have outlined but must also be able to recognize and pose the critical problems to solve tomorrow. We cannot tell students just what problems they will face in the future. They must learn to define the problems and create new mathematics with which to tackle them. These skills can begin to be developed as early as preschool, and this development should continue throughout one's life.

HOW MIGHT WE FIND AND/OR CREATE GOOD PROBLEMS TO EXPLORE?

If we wish students to become proficient problem solvers and to move from there to becoming the posers of interesting mathematical problems and the creators of new mathematics, we must provide them with multiple opportunities to work on interesting mathematical investigations. The following is a list of criteria for recognizing and developing this type of investigation or problem:

1. Tasks should ask questions that make students think, not questions that make them guess what the teacher is thinking.

2. Tasks should enable children to build on previous knowledge and to discover previously unknown mathematical principles and concepts.

3. Tasks should be rich, with a wide range of opportunities for children to explore, reflect, extend, and branch out into new related areas.

4. Tasks should give children the opportunity to demonstrate abilities on a variety of levels and in a variety of ways, verbally, geometrically, graphically, algebraically, numerically, and so on. Try scaffolding the questions, so every child can be successful on some level while maintaining a high level of challenge for children who are ready and eager to progress. Scaffolding means that a problem might have several parts, beginning with a relatively simple question that all children should have success answering and then building to more complex questions that challenge even the most skillful students. In this way, all students can be working on the same basic problem at an appropriate level, much in the same way that students might all be writing a story on the same theme but writing it on widely different levels.

5. Tasks should allow children to use their abilities to question, reason, communicate, solve problems, and make connections to other areas of mathematics as well as to other subject areas and real world problems.

6. Tasks should make full, APPROPRIATE use of technology such as calculators and computers as well as mathematical manipulatives and models.

7. Tasks should give time for individual reflection and problem solving as well as time for group exploration and discovery.

8. Tasks should be interesting and should actively involve the child.

9. Tasks should be open, with more than one right answer and/or more than one path to solution.

10. Tasks should encourage continued exploration once the initial question has been answered. One problem should be a springboard for several others. Teachers should work on these problems with colleagues before trying them with students to see how many solutions, patterns, generalizations, and related problems they can find themselves.

Figure 1.1. Open-Approach Heuristic

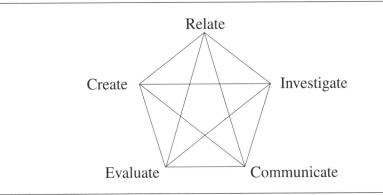

WHAT MODELS MIGHT WE USE TO INCREASE THE NUMBERS AND LEVELS OF MATHEMATICALLY PROMISING STUDENTS?

One way to begin to develop this mathematical potential is to teach students to use an open-approach heuristic such as the one shown in Figure 1.1.

In this model, students might start anywhere and proceed in a non-linear fashion to creatively investigate a problem. For example, a student might relate ideas about solving this problem to previous problems that they have solved, investigate those ideas, create new problems to work on, evaluate solutions, communicate the results, and think of other related problems to work on. Problems suggested in this book will show students ways to delve deeply into interesting problems in this manner.

Note that in this model, students do not stop when they have found a solution. Too often, students are satisfied with getting an answer to a problem and not looking at it any further. In this way, they miss the excitement of thinking deeply about mathematical ideas and discovering new concepts. Students need to learn to explore problems to find that the fun has only just begun when the original problem has been solved. Mathematicians will tell you that the real mathematics begins after a solution has been found.

This model gets away from the traditional question of mathematics for gifted and talented students that asked whether students' mathematical experiences should be enriched (often meaning adding additional topics to the curriculum) or accelerated (often meaning going through the traditional curriculum more quickly).

Following the Third International Mathematics and Science study, one frequently heard comments about the mathematics curriculum in the United States as being "an inch deep and a mile wide" (Schmidt, McKnight, & Raizen, 1996). Mathematics textbooks in the United States

8   EXTENDING THE
    CHALLENGE IN
    MATHEMATICS

Figure 1.2. Model for Adding Depth and Complexity to the Mathematics Curriculum

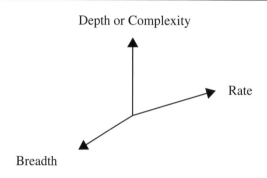

tend to cover large numbers of topics at a relatively shallow level and repeat the same topics for years. For example, it is not uncommon to see children studying whole number addition with regrouping each year from first grade through sixth grade (and sometimes even later). Whole number addition is often one of a hundred or more topics that students encounter in a mathematics class each year. Given the already large number of topics and the shallow level of coverage, it makes more sense to think of a mathematical model of instruction that is at least three dimensional, such as that shown in Figure 1.2.

In this model, an optimal level should be found for all three dimensions, but it is more critical to add depth and complexity to the study of mathematics rather than to focus on the addition of "enrichment" topics to broaden the curriculum or to increase the rate of instruction at the expense of depth. Many students seem to think of mathematics as a topic to finish as quickly as possible rather than one to enjoy and savor. As I hope you will experience as you work through the problems in this book, mathematics is much more enjoyable when you learn to follow the motto of Professor Arnold Ross of Ohio State: "Think deeply about simple things." Professor Ross has worked with many of the greatest mathematical thinkers in the United States at the high school, college, and graduate level for over 60 years. His greatest legacy may be that he has taught students that the most complex and enjoyable mathematical explorations begin with simple concepts that they mine for their richness and elegance.

Problems presented in this book will often use some of the following questions to help students learn to explore problems in depth.

Organization and Representation

1. How might I represent, simulate, model, or visualize these ideas in various ways?

2. How might I sort, organize, and present this information?

3. What patterns do I see in this data?

Rules and Procedures

1. What steps might I follow to solve that? Are they reversible? Is there an easier or better way?

2. Do I have enough information? Too much information? Conflicting information?

Optimization and Measurement

1. How big is it?

2. What is the largest possible answer? The smallest?

3. How many solutions are possible? Which is the best?

4. What are the chances? What is the best chance?

Reasoning and Verification

1. Why does that work? If it does not work, why not?

2. Will that always work? Will that ever work?

3. Is that reasonable? Can you prove that? Are you sure?

As students begin to explore problems in depth, they should also realize that answering the original question is just the beginning. The real mathematics often starts after the original question has been answered. Creative mathematicians learn to question the answers; they don't just answer the questions. In this book, to encourage students to become problem posers and creators of new mathematics, they will be encouraged to ask several of the following questions:

Generalizations

1. What other patterns do I notice?

2. Can I generalize these patterns?

3. Are there exceptions to my rules? Under what conditions does this work or not work?

Comparisons and Relationships

1. How is this like other mathematical problems or patterns that I have seen?

2. How does it differ? What other questions does this raise?

3. How does this relate to real-life situations or models?

4. How are two factors or variables related? What new relationships can I find?

5. What if I change one or more parts of the problem? How does that affect the outcomes? (Adapted from Sheffield, February 2000, p. 419)

With questions such as these, the solution to the original problem is used as a springboard to deeper, more original mathematical thinking.

HOW SHOULD WE ASSESS SUCCESS?

If we wish students to become problem posers and creators of mathematics, we must change our traditional methods of assessment. This type of mathematical exploration cannot be evaluated using a multiple choice or fill-in-the-blank exam. Portfolios of student work that show progress over the course of a semester of an academic year are often a much better indicator of a student's development of mathematical power. We must also let students know that we are looking for depth of reasoning and mathematical creativity. Students themselves can help in the development of specific scoring rubrics for their problems and in analyzing and evaluating each other's work. The following are examples of criteria that might be used for this assessment:

1. Depth of understanding: the extent to which core concepts are explored and developed (this should be related to national, state, and/or local curriculum goals and objectives)

2. Fluency: the number of different correct answers, methods of solution, or new questions formulated

3. Flexibility: the number of different categories of answers, methods, or questions, such as numeric, algebraic, geometric, or graphical

4. Originality: solutions, methods, or questions that are unique and show insight

5. Elaboration or elegance: quality of expression of thinking, including charts, graphs, drawings, models, and words

6. Generalizations: patterns that are noted, hypothesized, and verified for larger categories

7. Extensions: related questions that are asked and explored, especially those involving why and what if

You may wish to use a rubric such as the one shown in Table 1.1 to evaluate some of the students' major mathematics projects.

TABLE 1.1 Problem Posing and Creativity

Scores

Assessment Criteria	1	2	3	4
Depth of Understanding	Little or no understanding	Partial under-standing; minor mathematical errors	Good under-standing; mathematically correct	In-depth under-standing; well-developed ideas
Fluency	One incomplete or unworkable approach	At least one appropriate approach or related question	At least two appropriate approaches or good related questions	Several appropriate approaches or new related questions
Flexibility		All approaches use the same method (e.g., all graphs, all alge-braic equations, etc.)	At least two meth-ods of solution (e.g., geometric, graphical, alge-braic, physical modeling)	Several methods of solution (e.g., geometric, graph-ical, algebraic, physical modeling)
Originality	Method may be different but does not lead to a solution	Method will lead to a solution but is fairly common	Unusual, workable method used by only a few students	Unique, insightful method used only by one or two students
Elaboration or Elegance	Little or no appropriate explanation given	Explanation is un-derstandable but may be unclear in some places	Clear explanation using correct mathematical terms	Clear, concise, precise explana-tions making good use of graphs, charts, models, or equations
Generalizations and Reasoning	No generalizations made, or they are incorrect and rea-soning is unclear	At least one correct generali-zation made; may not be well sup-ported with clear reasoning	At least one well-made, supported generalization, or more than one correct but un-supported generalization	Several well-supported gen-eralizations; clear reasoning
Extensions	None included, or extensions are not mathematical	At least one related mathe-matical question appropriately explored	One related ques-tion explored in depth, or more than one appropriately explored	More than one related question explored in depth

SOURCE: Sheffield (February 2000, p. 419). Used with permission of the National Council of Teachers of Mathematics. © 2000.

STRUCTURE OF THE ACTIVITIES IN THIS BOOK

In Chapters 2 through 5, you will find a variety of activities designed to encourage students to explore each of the content strands from the NCTM *Principles and Standards for School Mathematics* (2000):

- Chapter 2: Number and Operations
- Chapter 3: Algebra
- Chapter 4: Geometry and Measurement
- Chapter 5: Data Analysis and Probability

In each of these chapters, you will find activities suggested for Level A (generally novices or students from prekindergarten through Grade 2), for Level B (generally intermediate students who have some experience with the Level A investigation or students in Grades 3 through 5), and for Level C (generally students who have mastered the Level A and Level B investigations and are ready to move on to more sophisticated generalizations, perhaps using algebra, or students in Grades 6 through 8). These grade levels are simply a suggestion for a starting point. As you work through these activities with the students, you may find that students at one of the upper-grade levels do not have the prerequisite understanding to begin at the suggested level for that grade, and you may wish to begin with activities that have been suggested for an earlier level. You probably also will find that some of your students are capable of going far beyond the suggested activities for a given grade level. Feel free to adapt the activities to meet the needs of the students in your own classroom. You should develop probing questions to follow up on new student discoveries and encourage the students to do the same as they learn to investigate problems on a deeper level.

Activities have been designed to encourage the students to become problem posers and creators of mathematics. You should introduce the open problem-solving heuristic (see Figure 1.1) to students. You will find a reproducible form of this (Form 1.1) at the end of the chapter that you may wish to make into a transparency for an overhead projector or enlarge for a poster to post where students can be reminded of this process. Please remember that even though the activities are introduced in a fixed order, actual student explorations may proceed in very different orders as students investigate questions of interest to themselves.

Start at any point on the diagram and proceed in any order.

- Relate the problem to other problems that you have solved. How is this similar to other mathematical ideas that you have seen? How is it different?
- Investigate the problem. Think deeply and ask questions.

- Evaluate your findings. Did you answer the question? Does the answer make sense?

- Communicate your results. How can you best let others know what you have discovered?

- Create new questions to explore. What else would you like to find out about this topic? Start a new investigation.

You may need to simplify some of the language for very young children when you first begin this process, but even very young children have a strong natural curiosity that will aid them in the development of this mathematically powerful technique.

You should also copy Form 1.2, Questions! Questions! Questions! at the end of this chapter for the students and post it in the classroom. This will remind them of questions to ask as they investigate the problems. Once students are proficient at this, they should begin to investigate many ideas that you as a teacher may not have explored before. Don't be alarmed if they ask questions that you cannot answer. This is a great sign that students are indeed learning to "think deeply." If you and the students get stuck in an investigation, don't forget that there are often great resources available as nearby as your computer. At the end of the book, you will find a list of resources for additional problems and for "expert" mathematicians who are willing to help you in your investigations.

Each of the investigations in Chapters 2 through 5 will be presented in the same format with the following sections:

Relate. Here the stage is set for the investigation by connecting it to the NCTM *Principles and Standards* and prior mathematical learning. Mention is also made here of routine exercises that may be encountered in a traditional mathematics program that address these same topics on a less challenging level. These investigations may often be substituted for those parts of the textbook, thus freeing more time for complex, thought-provoking explorations.

Investigate. This is the initial problem to start the students thinking about the investigation. There will be a reproducible form to accompany this problem that can be copied and given to the students. This section also will include suggestions for the teacher that will be needed to get started.

Evaluate and Communicate. This section includes ideas for the students to evaluate their own thinking and suggestions for probing assessment questions and responses for the teacher. It also includes ideas for the students for sharing their solutions. Correct answers with possible student discussion are included in this section.

Create. Ideas for extending and deepening the investigation are given here. These ideas should help even the most accomplished students to add depth and complexity to their reasoning.

Discussion. This section gives teachers hints on what to look for in students' solutions and ideas for encouraging them to dig more deeply into the mathematical concepts presented.

In the Resources, you will find a list of resources for other ideas for extending and challenging the thinking of mathematically promising students. These are designed to help you and the students continue your investigations and strengthen your mathematical power and enjoyment. Many of these make use of resources on the ever-changing World Wide Web. If students do not have access to these resources at home, you may need to help them find a way to use other public access to computers and the Internet either at school or in a public library. You also may wish to have a parents' mathematics night to explain your mathematical goals and processes and to let parents share in exploring the rich resources available.

REPRODUCIBLE FORMS

At the end of each chapter, you will find forms that you are permitted to reproduce for the students in your classroom. These forms should make it easy for you as a teacher to present the problems to the students.

As you begin your own explorations through this book, be sure to take time yourself to enjoy the thought processes involved in investigating new ideas. Let the students see that none of us have all the answers, but we can all take pleasure in the search for them.

Form 1.1.   **Open Approach to Problem Solving**

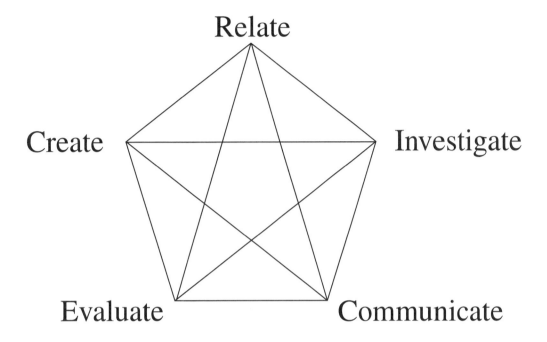

Start at any point on the diagram and proceed in any order.

- Relate the problem to other problems that you have solved. How is this similar to other mathematical ideas that you have seen? How is it different?

- Investigate the problem. Think deeply and ask questions.

- Evaluate your findings. Did you answer the question? Does the answer make sense?

- Communicate your results. How can you best let others know what you have discovered?

- Create new questions to explore. What else would you like to find out about this topic? Start a new investigation.

Form 1.2. Questions! Questions! Questions!

Think Deeply About Simple Things

- How might I model or organize my thoughts?
- Why did that work?
- Why did that not work?
- How is this like any other problem I have solved?
- How is this different from other problems?
- Is that always true?
- Will that ever work?
- What patterns do I notice?
- What is the largest possible answer? The smallest?
- How many solutions are possible?
- How might I best convince others of my results?

Question the Answers: Don't Just Answer the Questions

- What other questions came up as I solved the original problem?
- What if I changed part of the problem?
- What if part of the problem were not there or a new part were added?
- Can I do that another way? How many ways might I . . . ?
- What other patterns do I notice?
- What generalizations might I make? Are they always true?
- What other problems might I solve in a similar way?

Number and Operations 2

Investigations in this chapter will focus on developing a student's sense of number and operations such as addition, subtraction, multiplication, and division with whole and rational numbers, and using this sense to build fluency and power with computation. In all explorations, students are asked to make conjectures and test their hypotheses using a variety of strategies. Activities make use of the heuristic and questioning strategies outlined in Chapter 1, and teachers and students are encouraged to build on the investigations with other questions and explorations of their own.

All the investigations in Chapter 2 are related to the NCTM Standard for Number and Operations for Grades K–8:

Instructional programs from prekindergarten through grade 12 should enable all students to

Understand numbers, ways of representing numbers, relationships between numbers, and number systems

Understand meanings of operations and how they relate to one another

Compute fluently and make reasonable estimates (NCTM, 2000, p. 392)

You should work the problems on the reproducible forms yourself before reading about the solutions. In that way, you will get a much better understanding of the reasoning involved in the solutions. Remember, math is not a spectator sport. You need to be involved in problem solving before these techniques make sense.

INVESTIGATION ONE: HOW MANY WAYS?

Relate

NCTM Principles and Standards

- Compose and decompose numbers (break number into parts)
- Model place value and base 10
- Recognize equivalent representations for the same number
- Work flexibly with fractions and decimals

Prior Mathematical Concepts

- Count with understanding
- Recognize "how many" in a set of objects

Typical Textbook Exercises

- 7 + 3 = _____
- 47 = ____ tens and ____ ones
- 3 dimes + 2 pennies = _____ ¢
- 1/2 + 1/3 = _____

Investigate

A strong number sense is one of the most critical concepts to building a solid foundation for later mathematical power. Through the activities in this section, students will develop flexibility in representing whole and rational numbers and will begin to develop an appreciation for the power of our base 10 numeration system.

> **Level A—See Form 2.1 on page 33**

Level A, Form 2.1. In the beginning activity, students use markers on a ten-frame grid to determine the number of different ways that they can make a total of 10 using only two colors of markers (or two whole number addends). At this point, students are simply asked to record the total number of each color used and not to count different arrangements of those colors as different answers. (The number of different arrangements of 10 objects in a row with two choices for each object is 2 to the 10th power or 1,024. The number of different ways to get a total of 10 using two whole number addends is 11, a much simpler beginning investigation.)

Level B, Form 2.2. This investigation uses dimes and pennies to reinforce place value concepts of tens and ones. The ability to move from one representation to another, such as moving from coins to a chart to abstract numerals in the tens and ones place, gives students a solid foundation in our Hindu-Arabic numeration system. In this investigation, students should realize that the number of ones in a problem does not affect the number of ways that any numeral between 10 and 99 might be regrouped. The number of tens in the problem determines the number of ways that a number might be regrouped, which is always one more than the digit in the tens place.

Level B—See Form 2.2 on page 34

Level C, Form 2.3. In this investigation, students use fraction pieces to explore combinations of fractions that make one whole. Using only halves and fourths, students should find that they might use two halves, one half and two fourths, or four fourths. When thirds and sixths are added, the possibilities increase, as shown in Table 2.1.

Level C—See Form 2.3 on page 35

Evaluate and Communicate

Level A. After children have had a chance to investigate the initial activity, encourage them to discuss any patterns that they might notice. For example, it is much easier to find all 11 ways to make 10 with two different colors of markers if you systematically change one chip at a time (from $0 + 10 = 10$ to $1 + 9 = 10$ to $2 + 8 = 10$, etc.). Encourage the students to explain any patterns that they find and to discuss how the patterns help them make generalizations. The chart should help them organize their findings and guide their discussions.

Level B. The same type of systematic investigation that was useful in Level A will help students in the Level B part of this investigation. Students who are finding the number of ways to show 86¢ with dimes and pennies will find it easiest to start with either the smallest (0) or the largest (8) possible number of dimes and then systematically exchange coins, one dime at a time. For example, a student who begins at 8 dimes and 6 pennies might trade 1 dime for 10 pennies and next record 7 dimes and 16 pennies, and then with the next trade record 6 dimes and 26 pennies, and so on. In this manner, they should find that the number of possibilities is one more than the number of dimes.

- ⫞ ─────────────

TABLE 2.1

Halves	Thirds	Fourths	Sixths	Total
2	0	0	0	1
1	1	0	1	1
1	0	2	0	1
0	3	0	0	1
0	2	0	2	1
0	1	2	1	1
0	1	0	4	1
0	0	4	0	1
0	0	2	3	1
0	0	0	6	1

Level C. Students will find once more that the chart helps them organize their thinking to determine if they have found all possible combinations (see Table 2.1). Students may wish to use paper and pencil or calculators with fraction capabilities to determine if all their answers are correct. Many students will find that it is useful to record the number of twelfths (the least common denominator) for all these fractions when determining the number of possible combinations.

Create

Level A. The initial question leads to a variety of other investigations. Some students may simply change the total number of markers from 10 to another number and realize that the number of ways to get a sum of any given number using exactly two whole number addends is always one more than the given number. Some students may suggest a much more difficult exploration, and often they do not realize in advance how difficult a new investigation might be. For example, a student might wish to explore the number of possibilities for different arrangements of two colors of chips on the ten-frame grid in the original problem. Once they begin, they will probably soon realize that this number is an overwhelming one to attempt to list all possibilities (1,024). If they wish to investigate this, encourage them to begin with a smaller frame such as finding all the ways to arrange three markers (there are eight: RRR, RRG, RGR, RGG, GRR, GRG, GGR, and GGG). If students begin by finding all the ways for one marker (two: R or G) and for two markers (four: RR, RG, GR, GG), they may correctly predict that the number will double as each new chip is added. Another seemingly simple investigation is to determine how many different ways one can get 10 using exactly three whole (or counting) numbers. (Whole numbers are those beginning with 0, 1, 2, 3, . . . ; counting numbers begin with 1, 2, 3, . . . and do not include the zero.)

Using three counting number addends to get 10, students might realize that there are 8 ways beginning with 1 ($1 + 1 + 8 = 10$, $1 + 2 + 7 = 10$, $1 + 3 + 7 = 10$, $1 + 4 + 5 = 10$, $1 + 5 + 4 = 10$, $1 + 6 + 3 = 10$, $1 + 7 + 2 = 10$, $1 + 8 + 1 = 10$), 7 ways beginning with 2, 6 ways beginning with 3, and so on for a total of $8 + 7 + 6 + 5 + 4 + 3 + 2 + 1$, or 36 ways to get a sum of 10 using exactly three counting number addends.

Level B. Once students have found the number of possibilities using numerals between 10 and 99, it is natural for them to ask about the number of possibilities for larger numerals. Once numbers go above 100, students might suggest that the possibilities should now include using a dollar in the trades. If you wish to know how many possibilities there are using dollars, dimes, and pennies to show $1.23, you might first find that there are 3 ways using the dollar with 2, 1, and 0 dimes, and 13 ways using only dimes and pennies (with 12, 11, 10, . . . , 3, 2, 1, 0 dimes) for a total of 16 possibilities. In general, the number of possibilities for any number between $1.00 and $1.99 is one more than the number of dimes (using the dollar) plus 10 plus one more than the number of dimes (not using the dollar) for a total of 12 plus double the number of dimes. Students may find this generalization in a variety of ways and wish to continue to ever larger amounts.

Another question frequently asked by students is the number of possible combinations of any amount using any type of coins. Those problems will get away from the place value emphasis but will lead to a very valuable understanding of our system of money. Other students may wish to investigate whether the answers would be different if they explored the number of ways to illustrate numerals using the base 10 blocks rather than coins. They should find that using ten's and one's blocks gives the same answers as using dimes and pennies, and adding a hundred's block has the same effect as adding the dollar bill.

Level C. One of the most common questions that students will wish to explore is how the number of possible combinations is affected by adding additional fraction pieces or by changing the total that is desired. Adding eighths to the original chart keeps all the original answers and adds the responses shown in bold in Table 2.2.

This project could continue for many weeks as students find new questions to investigate. Students who have completed these investigations should have a very powerful sense of fractions, common denominators, naming equivalent fractions, and addition and subtraction of fractions.

Discussion

For many of these activities, students might wish to work in pairs or small groups to compare responses to see if they have missed or repeated any possibilities and to see if others worked the problems in the same way.

TABLE 2.2

Halves	Thirds	Fourths	Sixths	Eighths	Total
2	0	0	0	0	1
1	1	0	1	0	1
1	0	2	0	0	1
1	**0**	**1**	**0**	**2**	**1**
1	**0**	**0**	**0**	**4**	**1**
0	3	0	0	0	1
0	2	0	2	0	1
0	1	2	1	0	1
0	**1**	**1**	**1**	**2**	**1**
0	**1**	**0**	**1**	**4**	**1**
0	1	0	4	0	1
0	0	4	0	0	1
0	**0**	**3**	**0**	**2**	**1**
0	0	2	3	0	1
0	**0**	**2**	**0**	**4**	**1**
0	**0**	**1**	**3**	**2**	**1**
0	**0**	**1**	**0**	**6**	**1**
0	0	0	6	0	1
0	**0**	**0**	**3**	**4**	**1**
0	**0**	**0**	**0**	**8**	**1**

In this way, they develop an appreciation for multiple methods of solution and learn to expand their own thinking about a problem. These activities also are designed to develop students' abilities to organize and interpret data, find patterns, formulate hypotheses, and make generalizations from the results. These abilities will aid in the development of mathematical power throughout all mathematical strands.

INVESTIGATION TWO: SAME SUMS

Relate

NCTM Principles and Standards

- Develop strategies and estimation skill for addition and sub-traction

- Develop fluency with addition and subtraction with whole numbers, fractions, and decimals

- Understand the inverse relationship of addition and subtraction

Prior Mathematical Concepts

- Understand the meaning and effect of adding and subtracting

Typical Textbook Exercises

- 8 + ___ = 10
- 2 + 3 = 4 + ___
- 1.5 − 0.7 = ___

Investigate

The puzzles in this section are ones that can be solved by students of all ability levels, but these seemingly simple activities can lead to some deep understanding of the processes of addition and subtraction as well as properties of numbers such as even, odd, and multiples. Be sure to try the puzzles yourself before you read about these possible methods of solution.

Level A, Form 2.4. For the puzzles in this beginning section, students add three one-digit numbers to find equivalent sums. Some students will solve this in at least one way using trial and error, but it will be difficult to answer the questions about largest and smallest sums without analyzing the problem on a deeper level. This is a good problem for students to discuss in groups

Level A—See Form 2.4 on page 36

after they have had the opportunity to work on the problems independently. You may wish to pair up students who have found different solutions to discuss their findings. If students have difficulty analyzing the problem, ask them to determine the sum of 1 + 2 + 3 + 4 + 5. Because the number that appears in the corner will be used in both the vertical and the horizontal sum in the first problem, ask the students what the sum is of the three numbers in the horizontal row plus the three numbers in the vertical column. (That would have to add to 15 plus the number in the corner, which is used in both sums.) Because the total of the row and the total of the column must be equal, the sum of those two must be an even number. The only way to get the total to be an even number is for the number in the corner to be an odd number (15 plus an odd number is even; 15 plus an even number is odd). That means that the number in the corner must be 1,

3, or 5 and the sum of each row is 8, 9, or 10. Once the corner number is placed, the remaining four numbers are relatively easy to place; the largest remaining number must be in the same row or column as the smallest remaining number with the two middle numbers in the other two spaces. The same reasoning is true for the cross-shaped puzzles at the bottom of the page.

Level B—See Form 2.5 on page 37

Level B, Form 2.5. At first glance, these problems seem very similar to the Level A problems, using eight or nine numbers rather than five. It is important to realize in both of these Level B problems that there are now three or four corners that will each be counted twice, and four rows or columns that each must have the same sum. That means that the sum of all rows and columns must be a multiple of 4. The numbers from 1 to 8 add up to 36, and the numbers from 1 to 9 add up to 45. That sum, plus the three or four corner numbers, must come to a total that is a multiple of 4.

For the top puzzle, the multiples of 4 that are larger than 45 are 48, 52, 56, 60 . . . . To get a total of 48, you would need three corner numbers that add to 3.

Because the smallest total you can get is $1 + 2 + 3$ or 6, you need to start with finding three numbers that add to $52 - 45$ or 7. This might be done with $1 + 2 + 4$. Some experimentation will show you that the 4 must go in the middle because the 1 and 2 cannot be in the same row or column. Once the 1, 2, and 4 are placed, and you know that the rows and columns each add to $52/4$ or 13, the other numbers are not difficult to place. Students should explore to find other solutions.

For the puzzle at the bottom of the page, the multiples of 4 that are larger than 36 are 40, 44, 48, 52, and so on. To get a total of 40, you would need to have four numbers that add to 4, which is not possible. For 44, the four numbers must add to $44 - 36$ or 8, which is also too small, because $1 + 2 + 3 + 4 = 10$, so the smallest possible total is 48. That means that the four corners must add to $48 - 36$ or 12. This might be obtained using $1 + 2 + 3 + 6$. This will work as long as 1 and 2 are in opposite corners and each row and column adds to $48/4$ or 12. In a similar manner, students might notice that a sum of 13 in each row and column might be obtained by using four corner numbers that add to 16 such as 1, 2, 5, and 8, with 1 and 2 in opposite corners.

Level C—See Form 2.6 on page 38

Level C, Form 2.6. The puzzles on this page are classic magic squares. Students may wish to research the history of magic squares on the Internet or in the library, but they should first enjoy solving the problems on their own.

In the classic 3×3 magic square using the numbers from 1 to 9, if students only use a guess-and-check strategy, encourage them to ask themselves what the total of the three rows (or columns) is. Because each of the numbers is used once in the three rows, the total is $1 + 2 + 3 + 4 + 5 + 6 + 7 + 8 + 9$ or 45. Because each row or column must add to the same number, each must be 45/3 or 15. It is helpful to make an organized list of all sets of three addends that add to 15:

$1 + 5 + 9; 1 + 6 + 8; 2 + 4 + 9; 2 + 5 + 8; 2 + 6 + 7; 3 + 4 + 8; 3 + 5 + 7; 4 + 5 + 6$

Note that there are eight sets of three addends that add to 15, just as 8 is the total of the number of rows (3), columns (3), and diagonals (2). Ask students if there is a critical spot on these magic squares that is different from other locations, such as the critical corner positions in the earlier puzzles. In a magic square, the corner numbers each must appear in three different sums—one row, one column, and one diagonal. The number in the center must appear in four sums—one row, one column, and two diagonals. The numbers in the center of each side appear in only two sums. Encourage students to analyze the eight possible combinations above and relate those to the positions on the magic square. Only the 5 appears in four different sums, so it must be the number in the center.

In the larger square, the numbers from 1 to 16 add to 136, so each row must have a sum of 136/4 or 34. Students should be encouraged to find at least eight possible combinations of four numbers between 1 and 16 that add to 34.

Evaluate and Communicate

Level A. Students may be able to find one or more solutions to these puzzles without analyzing why these results are true. Discussing results with other students who have found different solutions should help them think about why the corner (or center) number is critical to these solutions and why even numbers will not work in those locations. They may need to be asked leading questions about the importance of the numbers in those positions if they seem to have trouble answering why some numbers work and others do not or why some solutions have larger sums than others.

Illustration 2.1. Student Solution to Same Sums Activity

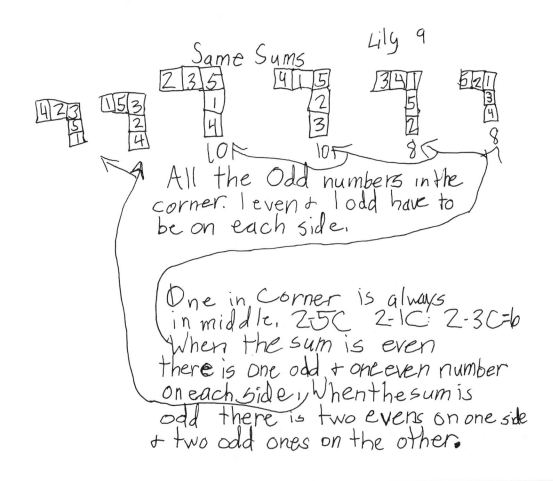

Some of the possible solutions are given here. Students may find others of their own. You should discuss what actually makes one solution different from another. Are they only different if the numbers in the corners are different, or do you want to consider them different if any number is in a different location?

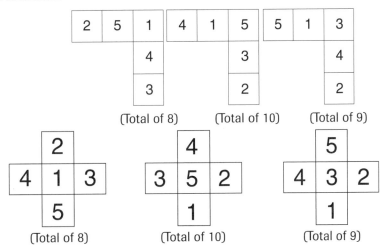

Level B. Finding more than one solution to these problems requires considerable analysis. A student who has difficulty in finding a single solution but is persistent in trying might be paired with another student who is usually successful quickly but gives up easily if a problem requires additional work. These students might share possible strategies and compare results. Other students who have found different solutions might be paired to compare solutions and strategies and look for additional ones.

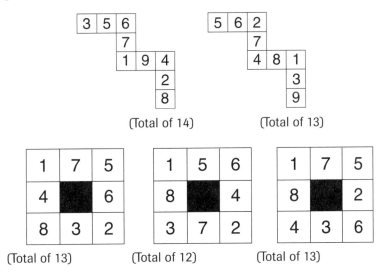

Level C. Puzzle and math enthusiasts have explored magic squares for over a thousand years, so be sure to allow students time to enjoy working with these on their own before they research what others have done with them. Students who enjoy these will find a wealth of similar puzzles to explore.

Possible solutions:

4	3	8
9	5	1
2	7	6

1	14	15	4
12	7	6	9
8	11	10	5
13	2	3	16

Create

Level A. After solving these initial puzzles, students may wish to explore what happens if other numbers are used in the same puzzles or if the cross or 7 shape is larger, perhaps using the numbers from 1 to 7 or 2 to 10. They should discover that the corner number remains critical to the solutions. Ask the students if anything changes if the sequence of numbers begins and ends with an even number. Some investigation should convince students that the corner number must be even if the beginning and ending numbers are even and odd if the beginning and ending numbers are odd.

Level B. Building on the Level A puzzles, students might change the puzzles by using the same shapes with different numbers or by enlarging the shapes. For the puzzles at the top, students might add more twists and turns to the staircase. For the puzzles at the bottom, students might enlarge the frame to one with four or five numbers on a side. Older students might wish to explore using fractions or negative integers.

Level C. Magic squares of all sizes make interesting explorations using whole numbers, rational numbers, and integers, and students can easily explore these for years. Students who expand their investigations to include historical answers to this question will find a number of other fascinating areas of investigation such as "magic stars."

Discussion

Some students will find it useful to have a calculator available for these investigations, whereas others might rely on mental computation.

Even those students who use calculators, however, will find that they become more proficient with computation as they work on these problems. These problems make interesting investigations for students at all levels. Students who need more practice with simple computation will receive more of this practice than they would in completing a number of worksheets, and students who are already proficient with addition will move on to higher levels of thinking such as analyzing data, looking for patterns, and making and testing hypotheses.

INVESTIGATION THREE: ALL IN A ROW

Relate

NCTM Principles and Standards

- Develop strategies for computation with whole numbers
- Develop fluency with whole-number computation
- Develop and use estimation strategies
- Use measures of center, including mean and median, and understand what these indicate about a data set
- Make generalizations about numeric patterns

Prior Mathematical Concepts

- Understand the meaning and effect of adding and subtracting

Typical Textbook Exercises

- Find the mean and median of the following: 2, 3, 4, 5, 6
- $7 + 8 + 9 = $ ____
- Is $34 + 35$ odd or even? ____

Investigate

Investigations in this section are designed to build upon concepts built in the first two number investigations, although students without that experience can still successfully explore these ideas. Students will build upon their sense of number and computation as they begin to explore deeper meanings of measures of central tendency such as mean and median and begin to use algebraic expressions to generalize patterns discovered.

Level A, Form 2.7. In this activity, students initially explore sums of consecutive counting numbers to determine which numbers can or cannot be the sum of two consecutive numbers. Once students realize that only odd numbers can be the sum of two consecutive counting numbers, they move on to explore the sum of three consecutive numbers. Students may choose to use a calculator for some of the larger computations. Encourage them to find a generalization to describe the numbers that can be written as the sum of three consecutive numbers. (All of these numbers are multiples of 3, and the middle number of the three consecutive numbers is the sum divided by 3.)

Level A—See Form 2.7 on page 39

Level B, Form 2.8. This investigation builds on Level A, as students look at a single number to determine all the possible combinations of sums of consecutive counting numbers that result in this number as the sum. Students who have determined that the sum of three consecutive numbers is always a multiple of 3 may be surprised to find that the sum of four consecutive numbers is not a multiple of 4, even though the sum of five consecutive numbers is a multiple of 5.

Level B—See Form 2.8 on page 40

Level C, Form 2.9. The chart used in this investigation should lead students to a number of insights as they build on the two earlier investigations. They should note that beginning with 3, every second number can be written as the sum of two consecutive numbers; beginning with 6, every third number is the sum of three consecutive numbers; every fourth number beginning at 10 is the sum of four consecutive numbers, and so on. They should also notice that the powers of 2 (2, 4, 8, 16, 32, etc.) have no solutions.

Level C—See Form 2.9 on page 41

Evaluate and Communicate

Level A. After students have discovered that any odd number can be written as the sum of two consecutive numbers and any even number cannot, encourage them to find a general way to describe each of the two addends. For example, if the sum is written as S, the first addend is $(S/2) - 1/2$ and the second addend is $(S/2) + 1/2$.

For three addends, the middle number is $S/3$, the first number is $(S/3) - 1$, and the last number is $(S/3) + 1$. Students might express this in a number of ways and should compare their expressions with each other to determine if they are describing the same pattern.

Level B. Students who have completed the Level A investigation should not be surprised to find that 84 cannot be written as the sum of two consecutive numbers but can be written as the sum of three consecutive numbers ($27 + 28 + 29$), and they may be surprised to find that it cannot be written as the sum of four consecutive numbers ($20 + 21 + 22 + 23 = 86$ and $19 + 20 + 21 + 22 = 82$). Encourage them to discover why this is the case. (Hint: Think about the middle number; there is a middle number only when there are an odd number of addends.) Students may wish to explore finding the sum where, if the first number in a sequence is n, a sequence of four numbers would be $n + (n + 1) + (n + 2) + (n + 3)$ or $4n + 6$. Because $4n$ is a multiple of 4, $4n + 4$ is also a multiple of 4, but $4n + 6$ is not. In a similar manner, students should discover that for any odd number of addends, any given number would be a sum of that number of addends if it were a multiple of that number. (That number will be the mean and median of the sequence of addends.) For an even number of addends, a given number is the sum of that number of addends only if it is a multiple of that number plus half of that number. (Eighty-four can be written as the sum of 8 numbers, because $84 = [8 \times 10] + [1/2 \times 8] = 7 + 8 + 9 + 10 + 11 + 12 + 13 + 14$.) Students who have made some generalizations about patterns of addends should be encouraged to share these findings with the class after everyone has had an opportunity to investigate the problem in depth.

Level C. The chart encourages students to organize their data and look for additional patterns. Students who have shared generalizations from the first two investigations should find those supported with this problem. It should be interesting for them to investigate why the powers of 2 do not have any solutions.

Create

Level A. Students may expand this investigation to other sums or a larger number of addends, but you should also encourage them to think about using a different sequence of addends. Perhaps they might investigate what would happen if the addends were consecutive odd numbers or consecutive even numbers rather than just consecutive counting numbers. Using algebraic expressions to describe their findings will help them generalize results.

Level B. Asking students to find all the numbers that can be written as the sum of 5 or 6 or n consecutive numbers encourages students to analyze patterns on a deeper level. Students might also ask what numbers can be written as the sum of consecutive counting numbers in exactly three or four or n ways.

These questions may lead students to discover that the sum of the first n consecutive counting numbers is $(n \times [n + 1])/2$. They may also wish to research the story of Frederick Gauss, a famous mathematician who discovered this property as a child when his teacher asked the class to find the sum of all the numbers from 1 to 100.

Level C. The chart in Level C should be extended to larger numbers to help students find the patterns, especially those for larger numbers of addends. For example, the smallest number that is a sum of 8 counting numbers is 36 and the next smallest is 44. Students may predict this from the numbers that do appear on the chart, but they may wish to expand the chart to check this hypothesis.

After exploring patterns from consecutive counting numbers, students may wish to extend this to consecutive even or odd counting numbers or use similar charts to continue explorations suggested in Levels A and B.

Discussion

The investigations in this section encourage students to develop mathematical power by asking them to make and test hypotheses and to begin to use algebraic expressions to describe their findings. Older students who have an algebra background should be encouraged to develop more formal proofs of their findings.

As students find unique and interesting patterns, be sure to give them the opportunities to share their findings with students and others outside the classroom. The Internet offers many opportunities for students to post their solutions to problems of the week on a variety of sites, and journals such as the NCTM journal, *Teaching Children Mathematics*, includes a problem every month that invites teachers and students to share their solutions and thinking.

Form 2.1.   How Many Ways?—Level A

Use red- and green-colored chips to fill all 10 of the following spaces.

Record the number of red chips and the number of green chips that you used. _____ red + _____ green = 10 chips

Again, fill all 10 spaces, but use a different number of red and green chips. Record all the possible ways to do this. Note that 4 red and 6 green is different from 6 red and 4 green.

Red		Green		Total
0	+	10	=	10

How many different ways did you find for a total of 10? _____
How many different ways would you predict for a total of 12? _____
Make your own chart and see if you are correct.

On the back, list two more questions that you would like to explore. Make predictions about the answers. Work with a friend to see if your predictions are correct.

Form 2.2. How Many Ways?—Level B

Using only dimes and pennies, predict the number of different combinations of coins that you might have for a total of 21¢. _____

List them all here. _____

On the chart below, list all the different combinations of coins that you might have for a total of 86¢.

Dimes	Pennies	Total
8	6	86¢

How many different ways did you find for a total of 86¢? _____
How many different ways would you predict for a total of 87¢? _____
Make your own chart and see if you are correct.
How many different ways would you predict for a total of 92¢? _____
Make your own chart and see if you are correct.
On the back, list two more questions that you would like to explore. Make predictions about the answers. Work with a friend to see if your predictions are correct.

Form 2.3. How Many Ways?—Level C

Using only halves and fourths, predict the number of different combinations of fraction pieces that you might have to total one whole. ____

List them all here. _____

On the chart below, list all the different combinations of halves, thirds, fourths, and sixths that you might have to make a total of one whole

Halves	Thirds	Fourths	Sixths	Total
2	0	0	0	1

How many different ways did you find for a total of one whole? ____

How many different ways would you predict for a total of one whole if you also have eighths? ____ Make your own chart and see if you are correct.

On the back, list two more questions that you would like to explore. Make predictions about the answers. Work with a friend to see if your predictions are correct.

Form 2.4.   Same Sums—Level A

Put the numbers 1 to 5 in the following squares so that each row and column has the same sum. Use each number once.

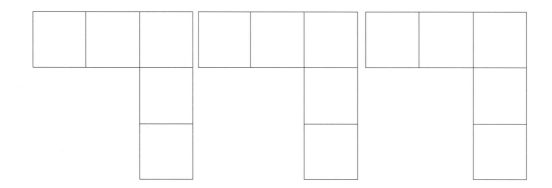

Is there more than one way to do this? How many different ways can you find? Do they all have the same sum? If not, which sum is the largest? Which is the smallest? Why?

Now try putting the numbers 1 to 5 in the following squares so that each row and column has the same sum. Use each number once.

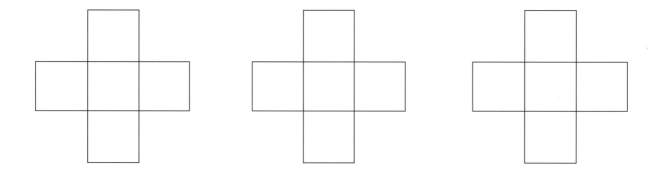

Answer the same questions as before. What did you notice?

Make up your own puzzles and give them to a friend to solve.

Form 2.5. Same Sums—Level B

Put the numbers 1 to 9 in the following squares so that each row and column has the same sum. Use each number once.

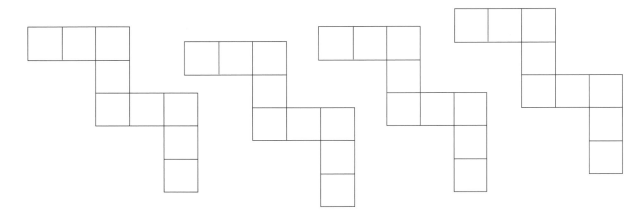

Is there more than one way to do this? How many different ways can you find? Do they all have the same sum? If not, which sum is the largest? Which is the smallest? Why?

Now try putting the numbers 1 to 8 in the following squares so that each row and column has the same sum. Use each number once.

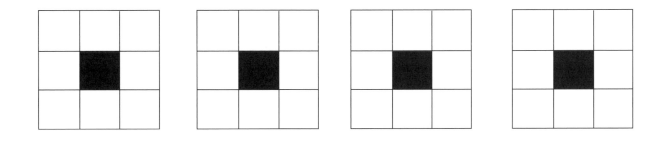

Answer the same questions as before. What did you notice?

Make up your own puzzles and give them to a friend to solve.

Form 2.6. Same Sums—Level C

Put the numbers 1 to 9 in the following squares so that each row, column, and diagonal has the same sum. Squares that work like this are called magic squares. Use each number once.

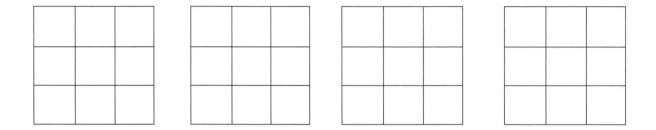

Is there more than one way to do this? How many different ways can you find? Do they all have the same sum? If not, which sum is the largest? Which is the smallest? Why?

Now try putting the numbers 1 to 16 in the following magic squares so that each row, column, and diagonal has the same sum. Use each number once.

Answer the same questions as before. What did you notice?

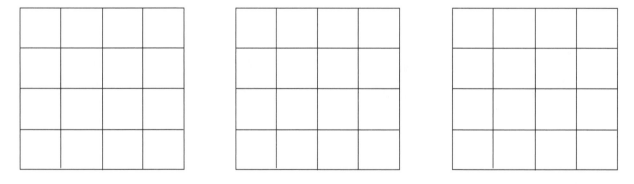

Make up your own puzzles and give them to a friend to solve. Look up information about magic squares and Benjamin Franklin on the Internet or at your local library.

Form 2.7. All in a Row—Level A

Find two consecutive counting numbers that add to each of the following sums. (Consecutive counting numbers are those that you say in order when you are counting. The smallest counting number is 1.)

15 = _____ + _____   18 = _____ + _____

57 = _____ + _____   58 = _____ + _____

229 = _____ + _____   228 = _____ + _____

What did you notice about each of the sums above? Were all of them possible to solve? Why or why not?

Now try the same thing for three consecutive counting numbers.

15 = _____ + _____ + _____   18 = _____ + _____ + _____

57 = _____ + _____ + _____   58 = _____ + _____ + _____

229 = _____ + _____ + _____   228 = _____ + _____ + _____

What did you notice about each of the sums above? Were all of them possible to solve? Why or why not?

Make up your own puzzles and give them to a friend to solve. Are any of your puzzles impossible? How do you know?

Form 2.8.   All in a Row—Level B

Eighty-four is the sum of consecutive counting numbers. How many different ways might this be possible? For example, can it be the sum of two consecutive counting numbers? Three consecutive numbers? 4? 5? 6? 7? More?

84 = ___+___   84 = ___+___+___

84 = ___+___+___+___   84 = ___+___+___+___+___

84 = ___+___+___+___+___+___   84 = ___+___+___+___+___+___+___

84 = ___+___+___+___+___+___ . . . +___+___

What did you notice about each of the sums above? Were all of them possible to solve? Why or why not?

Now try the same thing for 90.

90 = ___+___   90 = ___+___+___

90 = ___+___+___+___   90 = ___+___+___+___+___

90 = ___+___+___+___+___+___   90 = ___+___+___+___+___+___+___

90 = ___+___+___+___+___+___ . . . +___+___

What did you notice about each of the sums above? Were all of them possible to solve? Why or why not?

Make up your own puzzles and give them to a friend to solve. Are any of your puzzles impossible? How do you know?

Form 2.9.   All In a Row—Level C

As you have found, some numbers can be written as the sum of consecutive counting numbers. Investigate which numbers can be written as the sum of 2, 3, 4, 5, or more counting numbers by completing and extending the chart below.

Number	Sum of 2	Sum of 3	Sum of 4	Sum of 5	Sum of 6	Sum of 7	Sum of 8
1							
2							
3	1 + 2						
4							
5	2 + 3						
6		1 + 2 + 3					
7							
8							
9							
10							
11							
12							
13							
14							
15							
16							
17							
18							

Form 2.9. (Continued)

What did you notice about each of the sums above? Were all of them possible to solve? Why or why not?

Make up your own puzzles and give them to a friend to solve. Are any of your puzzles impossible? How do you know?

Algebra 3

Investigations in this chapter will focus on developing a student's sense of critical algebra concepts such as patterns, relations, functions, change, and use of symbols.

In these explorations, as in those in Chapter 2, students are asked to analyze patterns, make conjectures, and test their hypotheses using a variety of strategies. Activities make use of the heuristic and questioning strategies outlined in Chapter 1, and teachers and students again are encouraged to build upon the investigations with other questions and explorations of their own.

All the investigations in Chapter 3 are related to the NCTM Algebra Standard for Grades K–8:

Instructional programs from prekindergarten through grade 12 should enable all students to

Understand patterns, relations, and functions

Represent and analyze mathematical situations and structures using algebraic symbols

Use mathematical models to represent and understand quantitative relationships

Analyze change in various contexts (NCTM, 2000, p. 394)

Before giving the problems to students, you should work the problems on the reproducible forms yourself or with other teachers. Try this before reading about possible strategies and solutions. In that way, you will get a much better understanding of the types of reasoning, representations, and interconnections that might be involved in the solutions.

INVESTIGATION ONE: WHERE AM I?

Relate

NCTM Principles and Standards

- Describe, extend, and make generalizations about numeric patterns

- Express mathematical relationships verbally and using equations

Prior Mathematical Concepts

- Counting and skip counting

- Place value

- Addition and multiplication

Typical Textbook Exercises

- What comes next: 3, 5, 7, ___, ___, ___

- 42 + 24 = ____

- 1 + 2 + 3 + 4 = ____

- 4 x 5 = ____

- 19^2 = ___

Investigate

Even students in primary grades should begin to develop early algebraic reasoning concepts such as looking for patterns and expressing them in words and with symbols. In these activities, students will begin by using a hundreds chart to analyze patterns that build upon place value concepts and will expand these patterns to other rectangular and triangular patterns and generalizations.

Level A—See Form 3.1 on page 59

Level A, Form 3.1. In the beginning activity, students analyze a seating chart in the form of a hundreds board and make generalizations about locations of seats based upon the structure of the base 10 system. This is then extended to rows of seats with six seats in a row. In this problem, students may use multiplication or addition to generalize patterns found.

Level B—See Form 3.2 on page 60

Level B, Form 3.2. In this investigation, the shape of the seating pattern has changed from a rectangular one to a triangular one. This changes the pattern noticed from one based on place value or simple multiplication that adds the same number to each row (a linear function) to a pattern that adds an increasing number of seats to each row (a quadratic function).

Level C, Form 3.3. This again uses an increasing pattern of triangular numbers, but uses only even or odd numbers in this pattern. Students may wish to investigate the problems from Level A or B before tackling this problem, but even younger students or students without this experience can find a number of interesting patterns in this investigation.

Level C—See Form 3.3 on page 61

Evaluate and Communicate

Level A. In the first exploration, students should realize that Row 5 goes from 41 to 50 and Row 7 from 61 to 70. A seat that is two rows behind and four seats to the right of another might be found by adding 24 to the original seat number. In general, each row ends in 10 times the row number and begins with 10 times the row number minus 9 or 10 times 1 less than the row number plus 1. Therefore, the third seat in the row might be found by taking 10 times 1 less than the row number and adding 3 or by taking 10 times the row number and subtracting 7. Students might describe this in a variety of ways, and they should discuss their findings to determine if there are alternative ways of describing the same thing.

In the seating problem about the Highlands School, each row ends in a multiple of 6. Because $48 = 6 \times 8$, Seat 48 is the last seat in Row 8. A seat exactly two rows behind another would have a seat number that was 2×6 or 12 higher. Because this seat is two rows behind and four seats to the right, it is $12 + 4$ or 16 higher; $43 + 16 = 59$. Because the last seat in each row is six times the row number, the first seat is 6 times the row number minus 5, or 6 times 1 less than the row number plus 1. Therefore, the first seat in Row 9 is $(6 \times 9) - 5$ or 49. The third seat from the left in any row would be 6 times the row number minus 3, or 6 times 1 less than the row number plus 3. Again, students should discuss whether answers stated in different ways are equivalent.

Students should also discuss what makes the first set of problems about the Pleasantville School easier than the problems about the Highlands School, even though the second set of questions is quite similar to the first. The fact that the first set of problems uses a chart similar to a hundreds board and is based on our familiar base 10 system, should make those problems much simpler than the ones requiring knowledge of multiplication or skip counting by 6.

Level B. The Level B problems are more difficult than the Level A problems because each row adds one or two more seats than the previous row rather than the same number of seats each time, as in the Level A problems. Students should be able to determine that 15 is the last number in Row 5 by simply adding on to the pattern, but it becomes more time consuming to determine the seat directly behind Seat 42 by continuing the pattern. Some students will determine the first (or last) number in each row by adding one more each time rather than completing the entire row. They might see that the first number in each row follows the pattern of 1, 2, 4, 7, 11, 16, 22, 29, 37, 46, 56 . . . to see that 42 is the sixth number in Row 9 and then count up from 46 to determine that the sixth number in Row 10 is 51. Determining that the last number in each row is the row number times the next row number divided by 2 may take more guidance or experience. Some older students, especially those with some algebra background, may recognize that the last number in each row (1, 3, 6, 10, 15, 21, 28, 36 . . .) is a sequence of triangular numbers, and may recognize the formula for finding any triangular number as $(n)(n + 1)/2$.

Students should recognize that the seats in the auditorium for the Eastside School are simply double the pattern for the Glenridge School. To find Kyle's seat, they might simply follow the pattern of adding two more to the first number in each row and list the first numbers as 1, 3, 7, 13, 21, 31, 43, 57, 73 . Therefore, Seat 48 is in Row 7, and two rows behind Seat 43 is Seat 73 . . . Four seats to the right of that is Seat 77. Students who could recognize the pattern for the last number of each row for the Glenridge School should realize that because each row has double the number of seats this time, the last seat in each row will be that row number times the next larger row number. Therefore, the first seat in each row is that row number times the next smaller row number plus 1.

Level C. The problems in this section again make use of the triangular number pattern, but this time they use only even or only odd numbers. Students might find row numbers by noticing that the first (and last) numbers in each row again increase by an increasing number each time (this time by two more each time rather than the one from the first problem in Level B). The pattern for the beginning number in each row is 1, 3, 7, 13, 21, 31, 43, 57, 73 . . . , and therefore 65 is the fifth number in Row 8. This pattern becomes tedious, however, when finding the row for Seat 361. Observant students might notice that the middle number of each odd-numbered row is the square of that row number, and the two middle numbers of each even-numbered row are one less and one more than the square of the row number. Therefore, because 65 is one more than 8 squared, it is the fifth number in Row 8. Because $361 = 19^2$, it is the middle number in Row 19.

The pattern in the second triangle is similar, although now the middle number of each odd-numbered row is one more than the row squared and the square of each even numbered row appears just to the left of the center of the row. Observant students might also notice that the last number of the row is equal to the number of the row times the number of the next row. Note that these last numbers are the same as the last numbers in the second Level B problem. Students might explore other similarities between these two problems.

Create

Level A. Students might suggest an unlimited number of questions related to these seating charts or others that they have created. Questions based upon the chart for the Pleasantville School will strengthen students' mental computation and power with addition and subtraction as they determine the seat numbers for any location before, behind, or to the right or left of any given number. New charts can be developed with any number of seats in the row to strengthen concepts of multiplication and division of any numbers.

Students will also develop algebraic concepts of expressing functions using symbols, especially to describe linear relationships, as they express relationships noticed in words, symbols, and equations.

Level B. The patterns in this section are related to those in the Level B section of the All in a Row investigation in Chapter 2. Students might discover that the number on the far right of each row is a triangular number and is the sum of the first n counting numbers. This may lead to further investigations of other "geometric" number patterns such as pentagonal or hexagonal numbers or to a physical or pictorial development of triangular numbers. Students might wish to investigate actual patterns of seating numbers in local auditoriums and pose questions based upon these or their own seating charts.

Level C. Students should expand their investigation to look for other patterns on this chart. One natural investigation is to look at the sum of the numbers in each row. Notice that the sums for the first chart follow the pattern of $1, 8, 27, 64, \ldots$ (or $1^3, 2^3, 3^3, 4^3, \ldots$). In addition, the number (or average of two numbers) in the center of each row is both the mean and the median for the row.

Students who notice that the center number in each odd row (or average of the middle two numbers in each even row) is the square of the row number may naturally want to investigate why this is so. Because the total of all the numbers in a row is the cube of the row number and the center number is the mean, the mean may be found by dividing the total (r^3) by the number of numbers in the row (r), ($r^3/r = r^2$).

Discussion

This problem can be used as a bridge from the number problems in chapter 2 to the more algebraic problems in this chapter. It should be compared to the investigation findings from the All in a Row problems from Chapter 2, because once again the pattern of adding consecutive counting numbers might be applied to patterns in Levels B and C.

Students should find a number of additional questions, patterns, and comparisons as they work on this problem. Interesting findings might be posted on a class bulletin board, Web site, or newsletter to be shared with parents and other teachers and students.

INVESTIGATION TWO: HEADS OR TAILS?

Relate

NCTM Principles and Standards

- Recognize, describe, and extend patterns

- Represent and analyze patterns and functions, using words, tables, and graphs
- Model problem situations with objects and use representations such as graphs, tables, and equations
- Investigate how change in one variable relates to a change in a second variable
- Describe and compare situations with constant rate of change

Prior Mathematical Concepts

- Organizing data
- Simple graphing of coordinate pairs
- Counting money

Typical Textbook Exercises

- $(2 \times 3) + (4 \times 5) =$ _____
- Graph $x + y = 8$
- How much are a quarter, two dimes, three nickels, and four pennies worth?

Investigate

In these activities, students explore patterns of change using multiple representations, including physical models, charts, graphs, and algebraic expressions. The problems build the foundation for solving simultaneous equations by exploring these concepts on a concrete and graphic level.

Level A, Form 3.4. The first activity builds on ideas that were developed in the How Many Ways? activities in Chapter 2. Students explore a variety of combinations that satisfy the requirements for a total number of animals and a total number of legs.

Level A—See Form 3.4 on page 62

Before introducing the activity on the reproducible form, give pairs of students about 20 miniature marshmallows and 30 toothpicks. Ask students to use the marshmallows to represent the bodies of either chickens or horses and the toothpicks to represent the legs. Direct the students to build three animals that have the least number of legs. (This would be three marshmallows with two toothpicks in each for a total of 6 legs.) Then ask students to construct all the possible combinations of three animals and record the total number of legs.

Chickens	Horses	Total Number of Legs
3	0	6
2	1	8
1	2	10
0	3	12

After students are comfortable representing the chickens and horses with marshmallows and toothpicks, give them Form # 3.4, Heads or Tails—Level A, and encourage them to construct a model of the answers.

Illustration 3.1. Student-Completed Heads or Tails Activity

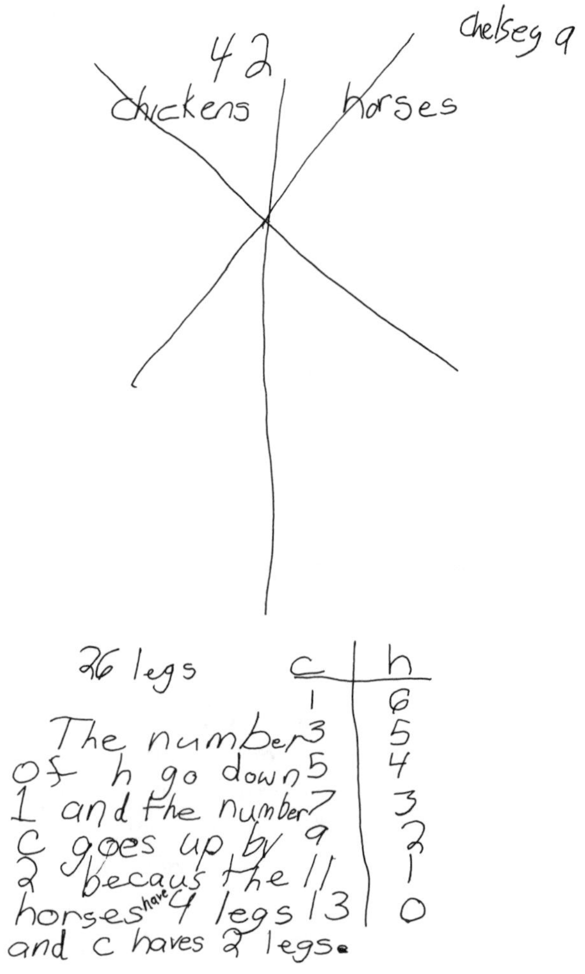

Illustration 3.2. Student Solution to Heads or Tails Activity

Forrest $9\frac{1}{2}$

- ~~Be resoureful~~, we were resourceful by flijing over pigs and turning them into something else.

- Every time I gave up a ~~horse~~ I had to get two chickins to maintain the amount of legs.

- $C+H=8$ H   C

  $3+5=8$ 5   3 $(2 \times C) + (4 \times H) = 26$

                          $(2 \times 3) + (4 \times 5) = 26$

                             $6 + 20 = 26$

Level B, Form 3.5. The investigation in Level 2 introduces students to graphing linear equations by plotting ordered pairs on a Cartesian coordinate graph. Students first graph all the possible combinations of animals that give a total of 8 and then graph all the possible combinations of animals that have a total of 26 legs. They should notice that five horses and three chickens appear on both graphs. Note that older students who have been introduced to solving simultaneous equations might compare this to graphing $C + H = 8$ and $(2 \times C) + (4 \times H) = 26$, and noting that the point of intersection (5,3) represents the solution to the two equations.

Level B—See Form 3.5 on page 63

Level C, Form 3.6. The Level 3 investigation expands to three variables: number, value, and weight of coins. Students may wish to use actual coins as they investigate these problems.

Level C—See Form 3.6 on page 65

Evaluate and Communicate

Level A. As students construct models of chickens and horses out of marshmallows and toothpicks, they should discuss any patterns that they observe and record their findings in an organized list or on a chart. Students who have completed the How Many Ways? activity should have no difficulty listing the nine possible combinations of chickens and horses for eight animals, and predicting that there are $N + 1$ combinations for N animals.

On the basis of the number of legs, the greatest number of horses possible is the number of legs divided by 4 (ignoring the remainder if there is one). That number plus 1 gives the number of possible combinations, because you may determine the number of possible combinations by first determining the greatest possible number of horses and then decreasing that number by 1 each time as the number of chickens increases by 2.

Level B. Students should record their answers in an organized list or on a chart before graphing the ordered pairs of chickens and horses. Note that the graphs should be scatter plots rather than line graphs, because the points on a line between the ordered pairs would be fractional values that have no meaning in the problem with chickens and horses. Students should discuss the importance of the point (5,3) that appears on both graphs. This represents the intersection point of five horses and three chickens that solves both equations.

Level C. Students should realize that with eight coins totaling 28¢, there must be a minimum of three pennies. That leaves 25¢ and five coins. Because five pennies only total 5¢, the five coins must each be nickels. For eight coins totaling 80¢, students will probably first think of eight dimes, but this is not the only solution. They might also have two quarters and six nickels.

The problem with eight coins weighing 31 grams with a value of 91¢ introduces students to solving equations with three or four unknowns. Students might begin by realizing that there must be one penny, because if there were six pennies, two coins would have to total 85¢, which is not possible. Taking the penny out simplifies the problem to seven coins weighing 28 grams with a value of 90¢. Algebra students might wish to represent this with three equations: one for the total number of coins, one for weight, and one for value:

- $N + D + Q = 7$ (total coins)

- $5N + 2D + 6Q = 28$ (weight)

- $5N + 10D + 25Q = 90¢$ (value)

Solving the three simultaneous equations or using other methods such as guess and test will show that there are two quarters, three dimes, two nickels, and one penny.

Two pennies, three nickels, two dimes, and one quarter also have a weight of 31 grams.

For 56 grams, the greatest amount of money possible would be using all dimes, or $2.80. The least possible amount of money would use a large number of pennies. Eighteen pennies weigh 54 grams, leaving 2 grams for a dime. This gives a total of 28¢. Seventeen pennies weigh 51 grams, leaving 5 grams for a nickel or a total of 22¢. The greatest number of coins also uses all dimes (28) and the least number of coins uses 9 quarters and a dime (10). It is possible to use all numbers of coins between 10 and 28. One of the easiest ways to do this is to make a chart and systemically trade a quarter for two pennies and then trade two pennies for three dimes.

Create

Level A. Students might begin by creating problems about different total numbers of chickens and horses and different total number of legs but will probably soon expand to questions about insects and spiders or three-legged monsters. Adding a third or fourth type of creature with a different number of legs quickly expands the difficulty level of the problem.

Level B. Solving two simultaneous equations with two unknowns by graphing points on a Cartesian plane to find the point of intersection is a fundamental algebraic concept. Students might develop a number of questions to explore using this technique. As with the Level A problems, students might ask about different numbers of horses and chickens or they might change to other types of creatures with different numbers of legs.

Note that as students make up problems for each other involving two equations and two unknowns, it is very easy to make up problems that are impossible if the students have not begun with actual numbers that they have modeled for themselves using the marshmallows and toothpicks, drawings, or some other type of representation. Encourage them to discuss why some problems have no solution and some have multiple solutions. Students might wish to compare the impossible equations to the graphs that show scatter plots that are parallel or that have a point of intersection where one or both of the numbers are negative.

You should also encourage students to explore other everyday or mathematical problems that might involve two unknowns. These could be similar to the coin problems from the Level 3 investigations or could involve other ideas such as the following:

- Given the area and perimeter of a rectangle, find the length and the width.

- Given the total number of stamps on the envelope, the cost of postage, and the value of each type of stamp, find the number of each type.

- Given the total amount of money spent for a given number of items and the price of each individual item, find the number of each item bought.

You might look at a Pre-Algebra or Algebra I book for other suggestions.

If you have graphing calculators available, students might wish to use these graphing capabilities to graph two equations and use the trace button to find the point of intersection.

Level C. Adding a third variable, the idea of weight, to the number and value of the coins raises the level of difficulty significantly. A third variable gives a number of new areas to investigate. Students may wish to expand their investigations to include other problems with three or even four variables. For example, if they have constructed problems about length and width when given area and perimeter of rectangles, they might expand to problems asking for length, width, and height when given volume and surface area of rectangular prisms.

More experienced students who have solved simultaneous equations with two variables by graphing linear equations and finding the point of intersection may wish to explore using a graph with x, y, and z axes to graph equations with three variables. For three equations with three unknowns that have a single, unique solution, their graphs will intersect at that single solution point, but finding this point is not simple with the common technology currently available.

Discussion

Constructing problems similar to any level of the Heads or Tails problems is relatively simple if a student begins with the answer and works backwards to ask a question. For example, if a student uses marshmallows and toothpicks to make four horses and five chickens, that student might say, "I have nine animals with a total of 26 legs. All are either chickens or horses. How many of each is there?"

There are also several problems that might be created that have no answers that fit the situation. For example, if a student says, "I have a total of five chickens and horses with a total of 13 legs. How many of each animal do I have?" there is no solution. Students might wish to ask what other questions would have no solution. For example, with a total of five chickens and horses, the only possible numbers of legs are 10, 12, 14, 16,

18, or 20. For all investigations, exploring why certain answers would not work is often an even more interesting investigation than exploring why certain answers do work.

INVESTIGATION THREE: FIELD OF DREAMS

Relate

NCTM Principles and Standards

- Model and solve problem situations with various representations including objects and equations
- Represent variables as an unknown quantity using letters
- Express mathematical relationships using equations

Prior Mathematical Concepts

- Addition and subtraction

Typical Textbook Exercises

- $9 - 5 =$ _____
- List all the addition and subtraction fact families with a sum (or minuend) of 7.
- $x + y = 7$ $y + z = 10$ $x + z = 5$; Find x, y, and z.

Investigate

Using multiple representations, including physical models, patterns, and equations, students explore the field puzzles to determine which have one unique solution and which have multiple solutions. These problems build a concrete foundation for students learning to solve simultaneous equations.

Level A, Form 3.7 Students begin by initially exploring the numbers of combinations of children in fields that add up to 7, building on techniques developed in earlier problems such as Heads or Tails or How Many Ways? From there they move to finding combinations that satisfy the conditions in three fields, A, B and C. It helps if students have small markers such as pennies or bingo chips to move around on the fields to find the combinations that meet all the requirements.

Level A—See Form 3.7 on page 66

Level B—See Form 3.8 on page 69

Level B, Form 3.8 The problems at this level move to students finding combinations that satisfy the requirements of four fields, rather than one or two as in level A. Again, students should be encouraged to use small markers in each of the four sections to help them find combinations that work. Older students might begin to write equations with variables to represent the numbers in each area.

Level C—See Form 3.9 on page 72

Level C, Form 3.9 The difficulty increases in the Level C problems as students find that there are multiple solutions to some of the problems. Even older students might find it beneficial to use markers in each area as they explore these problems. Students should compare their answers with each other to determine if they have found the same answers. Students at this level should also use equations with variables to explain their findings.

Evaluate and Communicate

Level A. The first fields have eight possible solutions: (7,0), (6,1), (5,2), (4,3), (3,4), (2,5), (1,6), and (0,7). In the second problem, the only possible solution for the fields is that there are two children in Field A, seven in Field B, and nine in Field C. The third field has a solution of eight children in Field A, four in Field B, and three in Field C. Students might work in pairs to find the solutions and compare observations as they work on them. Note that the total number of children in the second and third fields is always 1/2 of the total of the numbers in the circles. If none of the students notice this, you might ask questions about the total number of students and the total of the numbers in the circles to lead students to this discovery. Discuss why this is true. (Note that the three circles add to 2A + 2B + 2C.)

Level B. Level B problems build upon observations and techniques developed with the Level A problems. Students analyze the numbers of students in the fields to determine the missing numbers in the circles.

In the first problem, Field A = 3, Field B = 9, Field C = 2, and Field D = 6, the missing number is 15 and the total is 20.

In the second problem, Field A = 3, Field B = 8, Field C = 2, and Field D = 9, the missing number is 11 and the total is 22.

In the third problem, Field A = 6, Field B = 4, Field C = 9, and Field D = 8, the missing number is 10 and the total is 27.

In each of these problems, there is only one possible answer, but students might reach this answer in a number of different ways.

Level C. The first field in Level C has multiple solutions. Fields A and D will always have the same number of children, Field C will have 7 minus the number of students in Field A, and Field B will have 16 minus the number of students in Field A. Thus, both this problem and the first problem in Level A have eight different solutions based upon Field A having 7, 6, 5, 4, 3, 2, 1, or 0 children. The total remains 23, however, regardless of the numbers in the fields.

The second problem is similar. There are several numbers of children that could be playing in the fields based on the number of students in Field A. Field A might have 0, 1, 2, 3, or 4 children, and based upon the number in Field A, the empty circle will have 2, 4, 6, 8, or 10. The total remains at 13, regardless of the number chosen for A.

Students should discuss why the individual numbers in the fields vary but the total remains the same. Using variables to represent the numbers in the fields, in the first problem, using A for the number of children in Field A, Field B has $7 - A$ children, Field D also has A children, and Field B has $16 - A$ children. Adding the numbers in the four fields gives the following:

$$A + (7 - A) + (16 - A) + A = 23.$$

In the second problem, using A to represent the children in Field A, Field B has $6 - A$ children, Field C has $4 - A$ children, and Field D has $3 + A$ children. Adding these together gives the following:

$$A + (6 - A) + (4 - A) + (3 + A) = 13.$$

Create

Level A. Students might create other problems using the same diagrams and different numbers or may change the diagrams, adding or subtracting fields. As students make up their own problems, if they put numbers in the circles without first determining those numbers from the numbers of children playing in each field, they will probably find that some problems yield multiple solutions while others have no possible solutions.

Level B. With four fields and five circles for the numbers of children in adjoining fields, students should experiment to see which puzzles yield unique solutions and which yield multiple solutions or no solutions. For diagrams such as those in Level B, the connection between Fields B and C is a critical one for unique solutions.

Level C. Students should explore other puzzles to determine which have unique solutions and which do not. The use of algebraic symbols allows students to analyze mathematical situations and structures on a deeper level than the concrete, manipulative level that might prove successful for them on the Level A and B problems.

Discussion

Individual puzzles might be solved by using physical models and guess-and-check techniques, but deeper analysis requires that students use variables to represent the whole class of solutions. This gives students a much deeper understanding of the algebraic concepts of using mathematical models to represent and understand quantitative relationships and of solving simultaneous equations.

Form 3.1. Where Am I?—Level A

The seats in the auditorium of the Pleasantville School are labeled as follows:

				Front						
Row 1:	1	2	3	4	5	6	7	8	9	10
Row 2:	11	12	13	14	15	16	17	18	19	20
Row 3:	21	22	23	24	25					

The rest of the seats follow the same pattern.

Chris is in Seat 48. What row is he in?

Tyler is two rows behind and four seats to the right of Seat 42. What is his seat number?

Ron is in Row 7. What is the largest number of the seat that he might be sitting in?

I am in the third seat from the left in a secret row. Give a rule for finding my seat number using S to stand for the seat number and R to stand for the number of the secret row.

The seats in the auditorium of the Highlands School are labeled as follows:

				Front		
Row 1:	1	2	3	4	5	6
Row 2:	7	8	9	10	11	12
Row 3:	13	14	15	16	17	18

The rest of the seats follow the same pattern.

Kyla is in Seat 48. What row is she in?

Tina is two rows behind and four seats to the right of Seat 43. What is her seat number?

Rita is in Row 9. What is the smallest number of the seat that she might be sitting in?

I am in the third seat from the left in a secret row. Give a rule for finding my seat number using S to stand for the seat number and R to stand for the number of the secret row.

Compare the two sets of problems. What is alike and what is different? Is one set harder than the other? Why? Compare the method you used to answer the questions with someone else in your class. Did you use the same method? Did you get the same answer?

Make up your own seating problems and trade with a friend to solve them. Do you both get the same answers? Did you use the same methods?

Form 3.2. Where Am I?—Level B

The seats in the auditorium of the Glenridge School are labeled as follows:

Front

Row 1:	1			
Row 2:	2	3		
Row 3:	4	5	6	
Row 4:	7	8	9	10

The rest of the seats follow the same pattern.

Bill is in Seat 15. What row is he in?

Maureen is directly behind Seat 42. What is her seat number?

I am in the last seat on the right in a secret row. Give a rule for finding my seat number using S to stand for the seat number and R to stand for the number of the secret row.

The seats in the auditorium of the Eastside School are labeled as follows:

Front

Row 1:	1	2					
Row 2:	3	4	5	6			
Row 3:	7	8	9	10	11	12	
Row 4:	13	14	15	16	17	18	19	20

The rest of the seats follow the same pattern.

Kyle is in Seat 48. What row is he in?

Tyra is two rows behind and four seats to the right of Seat 43. What is her seat number?

I am in the first seat on the left in a secret row. Give a rule for finding my seat number using S to stand for the seat number and R to stand for the number of the secret row.

Compare the problems on this page to those from Level A. What is alike and what is different? Is one set harder than the other? Why? Compare the method you used to answer the questions with someone else in your class. Did you use the same method? Did you get the same answer?

Make up your own seating problems and trade with a friend to solve them. Do you both get the same answers? Did you use the same methods?

Form 3.3.   Where Am I?—Level C

The seats in the auditorium of the Woodfill School are labeled as follows:

                                Front
Row 1:   1
Row 2:   3   5
Row 3:   7   9   11
Row 4:   13   15   17   19
Row 5:   21   23   25   27   29

The rest of the seats follow the same pattern.
Joe is in Seat 65. What row is he in?
Lou is in Seat 361. What row is he in?
I am in the middle seat in a secret row. Give a rule for finding my seat number using S to stand for the seat number and R to stand for the number of the secret row.

The seats in the auditorium of the Eastside School are labeled as follows:

                                Front
Row 1:   2
Row 2:   4   6
Row 3:   8   10   12
Row 4:   14   16   18   20
Row 5:   22   24   26   28   30

The rest of the seats follow the same pattern.
Kari is in Seat 48. What row is she in?
Terry is in the first seat in Row 10? What is his seat number?
I am in the last seat in a secret row. Give a rule for finding my seat number using S to stand for the seat number and R to stand for the number of the secret row.

Compare the problems on this page to those from Levels A and B. What is alike and what is different? Is one set harder than the others? Why? Compare the method you used to answer the questions with someone else in your class. Did you use the same method? Did you get the same answer?

Make up your own seating problems and trade with a friend to solve them. Do you both get the same answers? Did you use the same methods?

— IIII ————————————

Form 3.4. Heads or Tails—Level A

When Farmer Jane looked in the barnyard yesterday, she saw eight heads. All the heads were either chickens or horses. How many different combinations of chickens and horses might she have?

Chickens	Horses
0	8
1	7

How many different combinations would you predict for 12 animals? For 25 animals? For n animals?

Today, when Jane looked in the barnyard, she counted 20 legs. All were chicken or horses. How many chickens and horses might there have been today?

Chickens	Horses
0	5

How many different combinations would you predict for 24 legs? For 42 legs? For n legs?

List two more questions that you would like to explore. Make predictions about the answers. Work with a friend to see if your predictions are correct.

Form 3.5. Heads or Tails—Level B

Farmer Fran saw eight heads in her barnyard. They all belonged to either horses or chickens. What is the greatest number of horses there might have been in the yard? What is the least number of horses? What other numbers of horses and chickens might there be? Graph the possibilities on the graph below.

Farmer Frank saw 26 legs in his barnyard. They all belonged to either horses or chickens. What is the greatest number of animals there might have been in the yard? What is the least number of animals? What other numbers of chicken and horses would have 26 legs? Graph the possibilities on the graph below.

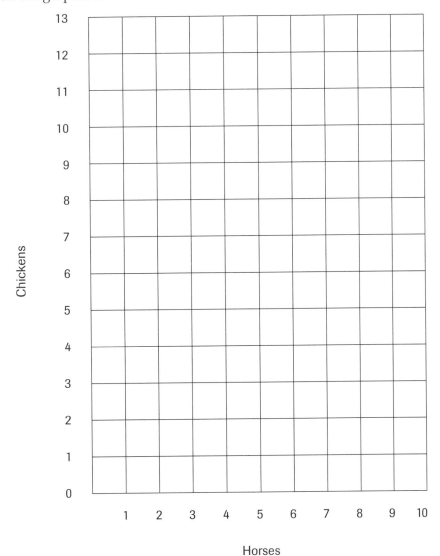

Form 3.5. (Continued)

When Farmer John looked in the barnyard yesterday, he saw eight heads and 26 legs. All the heads and legs belonged to either chickens or horses. How many different combinations of chickens and horses might he have?

Make up your own questions about chickens and horses. Work with a friend to answer your questions. Did you both solve the problem using the same methods? Did you get the same answers?

Form 3.6. Heads or Tails—Level C

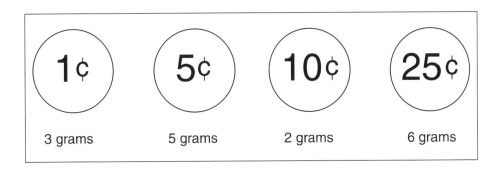

One penny weighs 3 grams, one nickel weighs 5 grams, one dime weighs 2 grams, and a quarter weighs 6 grams.

When Sarah counted the money in her pocket, she counted eight coins. She had 28¢. How many different combinations of coins might she have? What are they?

Jack and Jill each have eight coins that total 80¢. What coins do they have? Do they have to have the same coins?

Jack has eight coins that weigh 31 grams and have a value of 91¢. How many different combinations of coins might he have? What are they?

Eight coins weigh 31 grams. How many different combinations of coins might there be? What are they?

Jerry has a bag of coins that weighs 56 grams. What is the greatest amount of money that he could have? The least amount? What is the greatest number of coins he could have? The least number? What other amounts are possible?

Make up your own questions about coins. Work with a friend to answer your questions. Did you both solve the problem using the same methods? Did you get the same answers?

Form 3.7. Field of Dreams—Level A

Several children are playing different ball games in fields that are next to each other. On a fence around the fields is a sign with a number on it that gives the total number of students in the two fields. For example, this diagram shows that there is a total of seven students in Fields A and B.

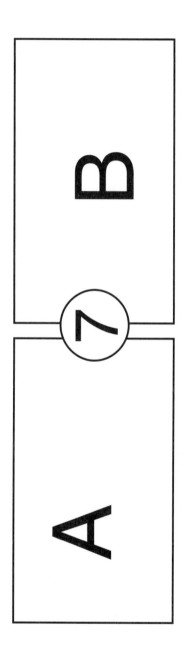

How many students might there be in Field A?

How many students might there be in Field B?

Figure 3.7. (Continued)

In the following diagram, there are three fields with signs telling the total number of children playing in the two fields next to the sign.

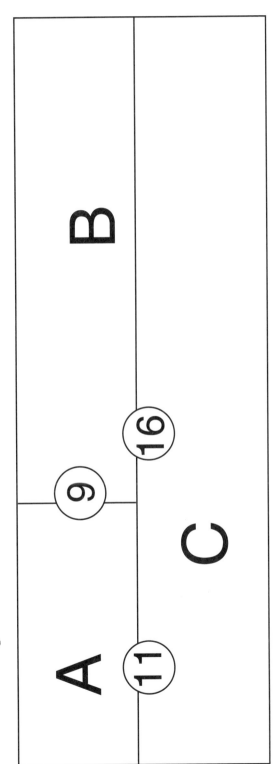

How many children are playing in each of the fields?

A_____   B_____   C_____   Total of A + B + C = _____

Figure 3.7. (Continued)

How many students are in each of these fields?

A ____   B ____   C ____   Total of A + B + C = ____

Make up your own Field of Dreams problem and trade with a friend.

Form 3.8.   Field of Dreams—Level B

Several children are playing different ball games in fields that are next to each other. On a fence around the fields is a sign with a number on it that gives the total number of students in the two fields. For example, this diagram shows that there is a total of 12 children in Fields A and B and a total of 5 children in Fields A and C.

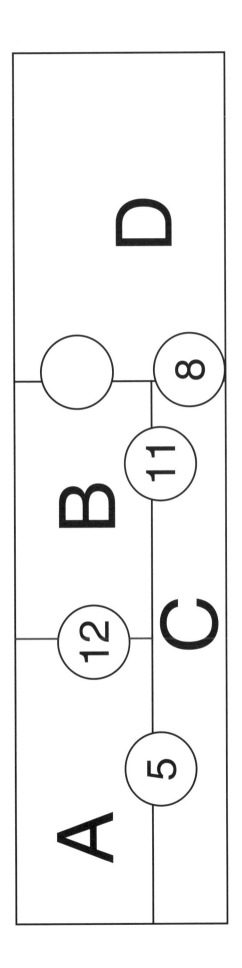

• What number should be in the empty circle?

• How many children are there in the four fields?

Form 3.8. (Continued)

Several children are playing different ball games in fields that are next to each other. On a fence around the fields is a sign with a number on it that gives the total number of students in the two fields.

In the following diagrams, there are four fields with signs telling the total number of children playing in the two fields next to the sign.

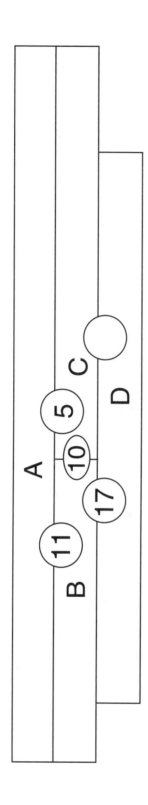

What numbers should be in the empty circles?

What is the total number of children in each of the fields above?

Make up your own Field of Dreams problem and trade with a friend.

Form 3.8. (Continued)

Several children are playing different ball games in fields that are next to each other. On a fence around the fields is a sign with a number on it that gives the total number of students in the two fields.

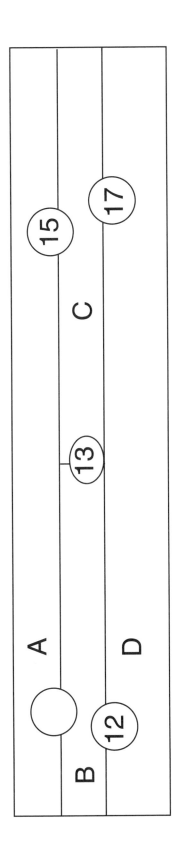

What numbers should be in the empty circles?

What is the total number of children in each of the fields above?

Make up your own Field of Dreams problem and trade with a friend.

Form 3.9. Field of Dreams—Level C

Several children are playing different ball games in fields that are next to each other. On a fence around the fields is a sign with a number on it that gives the total number of students in the two fields. For example, this diagram shows that there is a total of 16 children in Fields A and B and a similar total of 16 in Fields B and D. There is a total of seven children in Fields A and C and a total of seven in Fields C and D. How many children are playing in each of the fields? _____

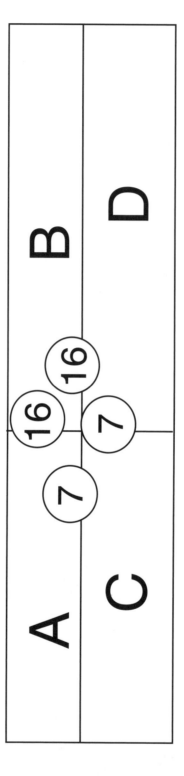

Is there more than one possible answer? Why?

How many total children are playing in the four fields? _____

Is there more than one possible answer? _____ Why?

Form 3.9. (Continued)

In the following diagram, there are four fields with signs telling the total number of children playing in the two fields next to the sign.

What number(s) might be in the empty circle? _____

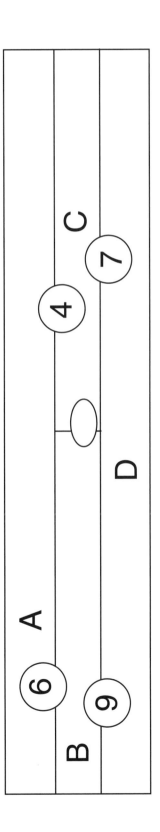

• Is there more than one possible answer? _____

• Why?

What is the total number of children that might be in the field above? _____

• Is there more than one possible answer? _____

• Why?

Geometry and Measurement 4

Investigations in this chapter will focus on developing a student's sense of geometry and measurement concepts such as analyzing attributes of two- and three-dimensional shapes and understanding what happens to measurements of a two-dimensional shape such as perimeter and area when the shape is changed in some way.

As in previous explorations, students are asked to make conjectures and test their hypotheses using a variety of strategies. In this chapter, students will be making and testing conjectures about geometric properties and relationships and attributes of measurement. Students will begin to create and critique inductive and deductive arguments about these properties, relationships, and measurements. Activities continue to make use of the heuristic and questioning strategies outlined in Chapter 1, and teachers and students are encouraged to build upon the investigations with other questions and explorations of their own.

All the investigations in Chapter 4 are related to the NCTM Geometry and Measurement Standards for Grades K–8:

Instructional programs from prekindergarten through grade 12 should enable all students to

Analyze characteristics and properties of two- and three-dimensional geometric shapes and develop mathematical arguments about geometric relationships

Specify locations and describe spatial relationships using coordinate geometry and other representational systems

Apply transformations and use symmetry to analyze mathematical situations

Use visualization, spatial reasoning, and geometric modeling to solve problems

Understand measurable attributes of objects and the units, systems, and processes of measurement

Apply appropriate techniques, tools, and formulas to determine measurements (NCTM, 2000, pp. 396–398)

Geometry has traditionally been one of the most effective areas in mathematics for building mathematical power in inductive and deductive reasoning and proofs. Investigations in this section are designed to build a strong foundation for this. It is important to work the problems on the reproducible forms yourself before reading about the solutions. In that way, you will get a much better understanding of the reasoning involved in the solutions.

INVESTIGATION ONE: FRAMED

Relate

NCTM Principles and Standards

- Describe, extend, and make generalizations about geometric and numeric patterns
- Explore what happens to measurements of a two-dimensional shape such as its perimeter and area when the shape is changed in some way
- Develop, understand, and use formulas to find the area of rectangles

Prior Mathematical Concepts

- Recognize and extend patterns
- Recognize the attributes of area and perimeter

Typical Textbook Exercises

- What comes next: 5, 7, 9, ___, ___, ___?
- What is the perimeter of a rectangle that is 5 feet by 8 feet?
- What is the profit on a book that costs $5 to print and sells for $12?

Investigate

The investigations in this section build upon the students' natural abilities and interests in recognizing and extending patterns. Students

combine geometric and numerical patterns to solve these problems. Problems begin with simple extensions of patterns in one dimension and extend to patterns in two dimensions. The Level C problems are more complex due to the addition of questions about profit.

Level A, Form 4.1. In this beginning activity, students analyze a pattern of tiles around the outside of a picture frame to determine the price. Beginning questions ask students to look at both the tiles in the interior and the tiles around the outside to help students focus on the relationship between the number of tiles and the cost of the frame. Students may see this relationship in a number of different ways. Some students will simply continue the pattern to determine how much Frames 6 and 26 should cost, whereas others may formulate a rule from just a few examples.

Level A—See Form 4.1 on page 96

Level B—See Form 4.2 on page 97

Level C—See Form 4.3 on page 98

Level B, Form 4.2. This investigation builds upon the patterns in Level A. Patterns in Level A extend in one direction as the picture frames continue to get longer. The picture frames in Level B get longer and wider, so the white tiles around the outside grow on all four sides. Students are again asked to formulate a rule that will work for any frame.

Level C, Form 4.3. This investigation uses the same frames as the Level B problems, but these problems add questions about other frames with the same area but different numbers of tiles around the outside as well as questions about profit. Note that rectangles with the same area often have different perimeters. If students found that tiles cost 50¢ apiece in the Level B problems, they should use that information in answering the profit questions at this level.

Evaluate and Communicate

Level A. Students will probably recognize quickly that the number of gray tiles in the frames is equal to the frame number and that the number of white tiles is equal to double the number of gray tiles plus 6. Therefore, Frame 6 has 6 gray tiles and 18 white tiles. Frame 26 has 26 gray tiles and 58 white tiles. The cost in dollars is half the number of white tiles, so Frame 26 should cost $29. Frame 15 will cost $18. Students might say that each white tile costs 50¢ or the cost is the frame number plus 3, or they might determine the rule in a different way. Encourage students who have different rules to discuss them with each other to determine if the rules are different ways of stating the same relationship. Students who have some experience with algebraic expressions might use algebraic properties to determine if they state equivalent equations. For example, a student who recognizes that the number of white tiles is double the number of gray tiles plus 6 might give the cost of the frame as $C = 1/2\,(2N + 6)$. Another student might recognize that the cost of the frame is 3 more than the frame number and give the cost as $C = N + 3$. Using the distributive property will show that $1/2\,(2N + 6) = N + 3$.

Level B. In the problems in Level B, the number of gray tiles is equal to the frame number times 1 more than the frame number. The number of white tiles is equal to 6 more than the frame number times 4. Therefore, Frame 6 has $(4 \times 6) + 6$ or 30 white tiles, Frame 26 has $(4 \times 26) + 6$ or 110 white tiles, and Frame N has $(4 \times N) + 6$ white tiles.

Frame 6 should cost $30/2 or $15, Frame 26 should cost $110/2 or $55, Frame 43 should cost 1/2 (4 × 43 + 6) or $89, and Frame N should cost 1/2 (4N + 6) or 2N + 3 dollars.

Again, students might find these solutions in a number of different ways and should discuss their different methods. Equations might be compared using algebraic properties to determine if they express the same relationships.

Level C. This exploration begins with a question investigating whether rectangles with the same area have the same perimeter. Note that rectangles with 12 tiles in the interior might have them arranged in a 12 × 1 or 6 × 2 configuration in addition to the given 3 × 4 rectangle. A 12 × 1 gray rectangle would have 30 white tiles surrounding it and would be priced at $15. A 6 × 2 gray rectangle would have 20 white tiles surrounding it and would be priced at $10. (Note that the number of tiles surrounding the gray tiles is not the same as the perimeter of the gray tiles.)

Students should work in small groups to determine different ways to find the profit for any frame. Some students will determine that the profit is 20¢ per white tile, and others may determine that the profit is 2/5 of the selling price. Therefore, for the frames pictured, the profits are $2.00 for Frame 1, $2.80 for Frame 2, $3.60 for Frame 3, and $6.00 for Frame 6. Frame 11 should have a profit of $10. Frame 96 should sell for $195.

Students who determine that the profit is 20¢ per white tile may find the profit as

P = 20¢ (4N + 6)

Students who determine that the profit is 2/5 of the selling price may find the profit as

P = 2/5 (2N + 3)

Note that using the distributive property shows that for both of these, P = $0.80 N + $1.20

Students may have different methods for figuring the profit, and they should be encouraged to compare their methods to determine if they are equivalent.

Create

Level A. In creating their own questions, students might follow the same patterns to ask about the cost of larger frames. Questions such as this encourage students to look for geometric and numeric patterns. Writing equations to describe the patterns also builds upon students' algebraic concepts as they relate functions, equations, and geometric patterns and physical models. Students should be encouraged to relate this to investigations from the algebra chapter, where they also wrote equations to represent patterns noted.

Level B. In this investigation, students explore patterns that expand in two dimensions rather than one, as in Level A. New questions at this level might expand investigations to a third dimension and ask questions about the surface area of a rectangular prism. Students might also investigate whether all two-dimensional rectangular frames with the same number of tiles on the outside would have the same number of tiles in the interior or whether all designs with the same number of tiles in a rectangular interior would have the same number of tiles on the outside. (They do not.)

Level C. Students who notice that different rectangles with an area of 12 square units have different perimeters might also explore whether this is true for rectangles of different sizes. They might also ask what shape rectangle has the greatest perimeter (a long, skinny one) and what shape has the least perimeter (a square). This information might be combined with information about profit to ask questions about frames of a given area with the greatest and least profit.

Discussion

This investigation builds on the problems in the algebra chapter as students continue to look for patterns and write equations to describe them. In this problem, the patterns are geometric, and questions lead students to explore connections between algebraic expressions and geometric, physical models.

As students write their own questions, encourage them to look for relationships between area and perimeter. Many students will assume that all rectangles with the same area will have the same perimeter, and this investigation should help them realize that this is not the case.

INVESTIGATION TWO: SHAPE UP

Relate

NCTM Principles and Standards

- Identify and classify two-dimensional shapes according to their properties

- Investigate, describe, and reason about the results of subdividing and combining shapes

- Predict and describe the results of sliding, flipping, and turning two-dimensional shapes

Prior Mathematical Concepts

- Recognize, name, draw, and sort two-dimensional shapes
- Describe attributes of two-dimensional shapes

Typical Textbook Exercises

- What is a square?
- Draw a parallelogram.

Investigate

In these investigations, students combine and subdivide geometric shapes to form new shapes. Problems in this section do not involve numbers; students visualize and manipulate geometric shapes, not numbers, to solve the problems.

Level A, Form 4.4. As students create new polygons, note that there are many different ways to name them. For example, a square is also a rectangle, a parallelogram, a rhombus, a quadrilateral, and a polygon. A triangle might be equilateral, scalene, isosceles, right, acute, or obtuse. Encourage students to cut out shapes and trace around them to record their findings with drawings as well as the names of shapes. Talk about different ways to classify the shapes created, such as by the number of sides or the perimeter.

Level A—See Form 4.4 on page 99

Level B, Form 4.5. Students should compare the numbers and types of shapes found in Level B to those found in Level A. Are there any shapes that can be made with two congruent right triangles that cannot be made with the addition of a rectangle? Are there shapes made with the two right triangles and the rectangle that cannot be made without the rectangle?

Level B—See Form 4.5 on page 100

As students find different possible shapes, they should sort them into categories (perhaps by the number of sides) so they can compare them. Ask them to determine whether shapes are different (not congruent) or simply a rotation or flip of another shape. Students may wish to cut out the shapes found and rotate or flip them over to determine if they are different.

Level C—See Form 4.6 on page 101

Level C, Form 4.6. People around the world have explored tangram puzzles for thousands of years. Students should find that they could manipulate these shapes into dozens of interesting designs to answer a multitude of questions.

Evaluate and Communicate

Level A. As students manipulate the two triangles, they should find that they could be combined to form the following parallelogram and two isosceles triangles in addition to the rectangle and parallelogram illustrated in the problem shown on page 99.

Note that the original rectangle has the least perimeter, the triangle on the left and the parallelogram from the original problem have the same perimeter as each other that is longer than the rectangle, and the triangle and parallelogram above have the same perimeter as each other that is longer than the other shapes. All shapes have the same area, because they are made from the same triangles.

Students should discuss their findings with each other as they explore combining and subdividing other shapes.

Figure 4.1.

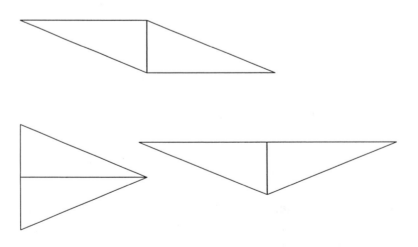

Level B. In combining the rectangle and two right triangles, students might find shapes similar to those found in Figure 4.2. Note that additional shapes are possible.

Note that although none of these shapes is congruent, they all have the same area. Perimeters differ, and students might classify shapes and order them from those with the smallest perimeter to those with the longest perimeter.

Level C. After exploring shapes formed with two right triangles and a rectangle, students should not be surprised to find the variety of shapes that can be made from tangrams. The examples in Figure 4.3 are a few of the ways to make squares.

Note that if the entire square made of all seven pieces has a unit of one, the small triangles are each 1/16 of the total. The medium triangle, the square, and the parallelogram each have an area of 1/8 of the entire square, and the large triangles are each 1/4 of the total.

Students should be able to find resources on tangrams either in the library or on the Internet and should be encouraged to share their findings with each other.

Create

Level A. Students might use a variety of polygons with different cuts to create congruent pieces to begin their explorations. Encourage them to be systematic in their explorations. Students who use only guess and test may have difficulty finding all the possible new shapes, but students who systematically flip and rotate shapes to fit them together should be more successful. Students working with partners or in small groups and discussing their results should be able to find all possibilities.

Level B. Students will find that the number of possible shapes made from combinations of three or more geometric shapes depends on several factors such as symmetry and congruence. For example, a square and the two congruent isosceles right triangles formed by cutting the square along a diagonal will form fewer different shapes than the rectangle and two right triangles in the original problem.

Encourage students to sketch, compare, and discuss their findings as they manipulate their geometric shapes.

Level C. People all over the world have explored tangram puzzles for thousands of years, and students should be able to find a number of resources to aid in these explorations. Encourage students to explore problems involving area and perimeter in addition to those involving spatial relations.

Figure 4.2.

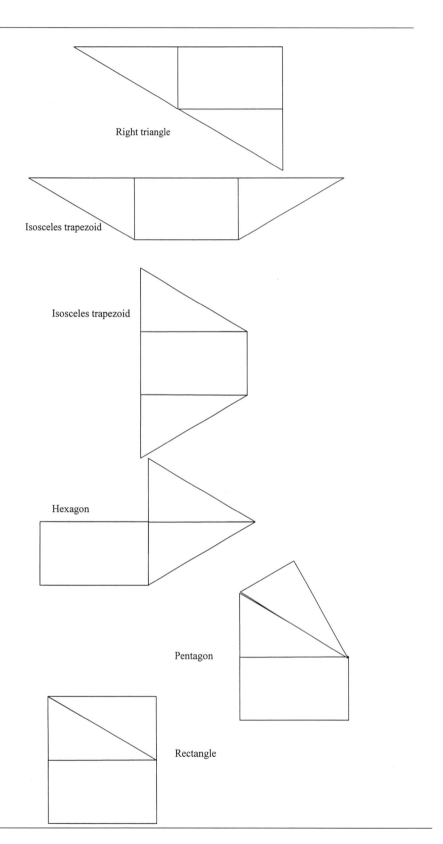

Right triangle

Isosceles trapezoid

Isosceles trapezoid

Hexagon

Pentagon

Rectangle

Figure 4.2. (Continued)

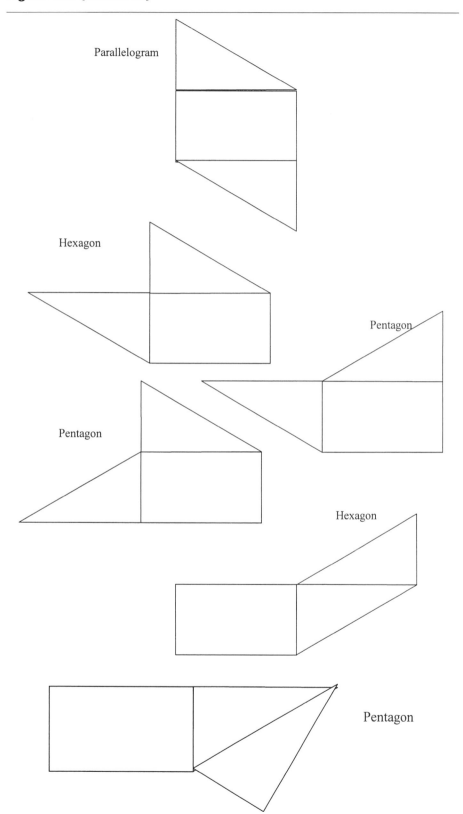

Figure 4.3.

Two pieces: Three pieces:

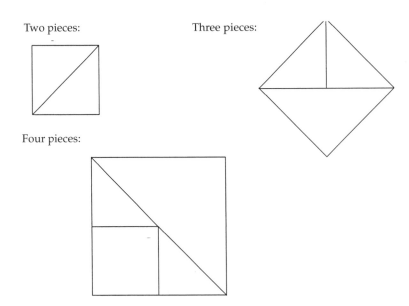

Four pieces:

Five pieces:

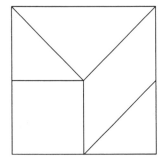

Six Pieces: It is not possible to make a square from six tangram pieces. Think about why this is so. Hint: If the area of the small square is one unit, what is the area of all seven pieces? (eight). Note that the side of the square below using all seven pieces is the square root of 8. The square above using five pieces has an area of four square units and a side of two. The first square using two pieces has an area of one square unit with a side of one, and the square using three pieces has an area of two with a side the square root of 2.

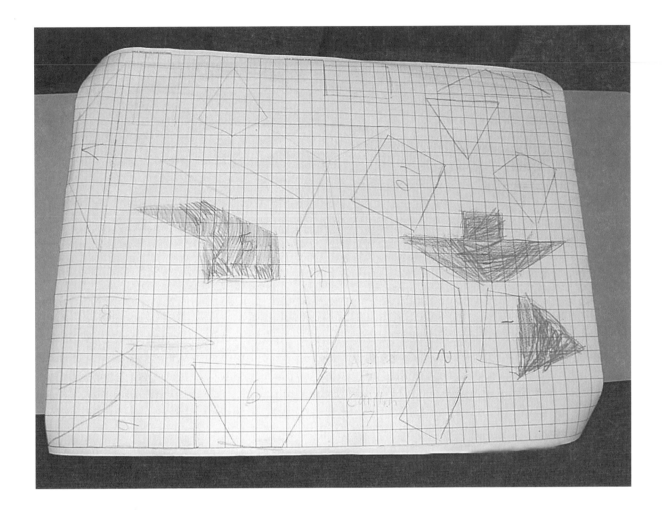

Students may enjoy reading *Grandfather Tang's Story* by Ann Tompert (1997) and solving the puzzles suggested there. Writing their own stories about the tangram puzzles that they create is also a very good way for them to develop both mathematics and writing abilities.

Discussion

Spatial reasoning and the knowledge of how geometric shapes are related to one another build a foundation for a variety of mathematical skills and concepts that do not rely on numbers or even words. Think about the spatial abilities that are required by a surgeon who is about to perform an operation or an astronaut who is preparing to dock with the space station. Students who have had numerous experiences solving all types of hands-on geometric puzzles can begin to develop these very important spatial talents.

Building these skills requires that students sort, build, draw, model, trace, construct, and visualize as they solve a variety of spatial problems.

Figure 4.4.

Seven pieces:

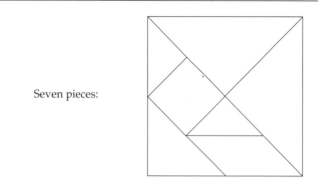

Throughout these investigations, students should be reasoning and making, testing, and justifying conjectures. Notice that students might use physical models and drawings to justify their conjectures; they do not need to use a lot of words. As students build, draw, and use physical models, their abilities to visualize, predict, and analyze geometric relationships will develop and grow. Frequently, children and adults have very similar abilities in these areas, because many adults have not developed these skills.

Illustration 4.1. Student Solution to Tangram Square Puzzle

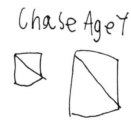

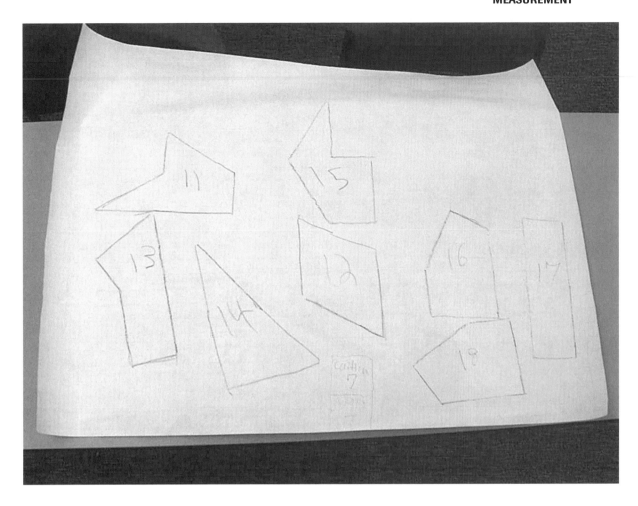

INVESTIGATION THREE: CONNECT THE DOTS

Relate

NCTM Principles and Standards

- Understand the attribute of area and select the appropriate unit for measuring it
- Develop, understand, and use formulas to find the area of rectangles and related triangles and parallelograms
- Create and critique inductive and deductive arguments concerning geometric ideas and relationships such as the Pythagorean relationship

Prior Mathematical Concepts

- Recognize, name, and draw two-dimensional shapes
- Understand the attribute of area
- Measure area using nonstandard units

Typical Textbook Exercises

- Find the area of the following rectangle:

2 inches

5 inches

- Name the following figures:

Investigate

In these activities, students use dot paper or geoboards to investigate patterns involving squares and areas. Students begin by exploring squares on squared paper with nine dots and make predictions about larger squares. The final investigation asks students to explore a variety of shapes on the dot paper or geoboard that have the same area.

Level A, Form 4.7. As students explore the possible squares on dot paper, they may wish to use physical materials to aid in their investigations. If you have them available, give students geoboards and rubber bands to work on these investigations. Be sure that students realize that not all squares will have sides parallel to the base of the paper or geoboards. They might use the corner of a sheet of paper or an index card to check to make sure that all angles are right angles and that all sides are congruent.

Level A—See Form 4.7 on page 102

After students have found the six squares possible on the 9 dots, ask them to predict the number of squares possible with 16 dots in a square. You might encourage students to use a chart or another method to keep track of the total possible squares and to look for patterns.

Level B, Form 4.8. In Level B, students extend their investigation of squares to the dot paper representing the most common type of geoboard, the one with an area of 16 square units or 25 pegs arranged in five rows of 5. Students are asked to determine the area of the squares that they find. This can be done by simply counting the square units in each of the squares formed with sides parallel to the sides of the paper or geoboard, but this is not as simple for squares with sides not parallel or perpendicular to these edges. To determine the area of these other squares, students should be encouraged to divide the squares into triangles or other shapes that can be used to find the area of the entire square.

Level B—See Form 4.8 on page 103

Level C, Form 4.9. The investigation in Level C builds upon the findings of the Level B investigation as well as the Shape Up investigations looking at a number of different ways to combine squares and triangles. In this investigation, students are asked to find as many figures as possible with an area of two square units. This builds a foundation for students developing formulas to

Level C—See Form 4.9 on page 104

find the area of rectangles, squares, triangles, parallelograms, and trapezoids.

Evaluate and Communicate

Level A. Using nine dots, students should find a total of six squares. Four of the squares have an area of one square unit, and one square has an area of four square units. The sixth square has an area of two square units as pictured below in Figure 4.5. Notice that this square is made up of four triangles that are each 1/2 of a square unit.

Figure 4.5.

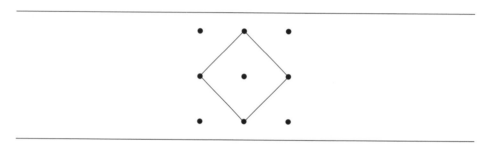

With 16 dots, students should find 9 small squares with an area of one square unit, 4 squares with an area of four square units, and 1 square with an area of nine square units. In addition, there are 4 squares with an area of two square units and 2 squares with an area of five square units, for a total of 20 squares. Note the square on the dots in Figure 4.6. Each triangle and the square in the middle have an area of one square unit (see Figure 4.6).

Figure 4.6.

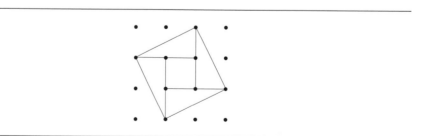

Students might find all the possible squares without finding their areas in Level A. These investigations will be expanded in Level B to have students find the areas as well as the squares.

TABLE 4.1

Area (in square units)	Number of Squares
1	16
2	9
4	9
5	8
8	1
9	4
10	2
16	1

Level B. This investigation builds on the concepts found with smaller geoboards or dot paper. Note that the square shown in the middle of the page is made up of four triangles, each with an area of 1/2 of a square, and has an area of two square units. Students may wish to work with a partner or in small groups to find the squares on the chart. They should get results such as those in Table 4.1.

Note that many of the numbers of squares of each size possible are also square numbers. Squares with areas of 2, 5, 8, and 10 are each found on a diagonal of the geoboard or dot paper. The length of the sides of each of these squares is the square root of the area. These lengths may also be found using the Pythagorean theorem. For example, note that the length of each side of the square with an area of 5, such as the one in Figure 4.6, is also the hypotenuse of a right triangle with one side with a length of 1 and one side with a length of 2. Using the Pythagorean theorem ($a^2 + b^2 = c^2$) to find the length of this hypotenuse,

$1^2 + 2^2 = 5$. The hypotenuse is therefore the square root of 5.

Level C. Figure 4.7 shows some of the possible polygons with an area of two square units. Students who have explored the areas of squares from the Level B problems may have a variety of strategies to find these new areas. Some of the areas may be found by subdividing the shape into whole and half squares. Others may be found by making a larger rectangle that surrounds the figure and then subtracting whole or half squares from the larger figure to find the area of the remaining polygon. Some students may know the formula for finding the area of a triangle (1/2 bh), a parallelogram (bh), or a trapezoid (1/2 [$b_1 + b_2$] h) and may use this formula to find the area.

Figure 4.7.

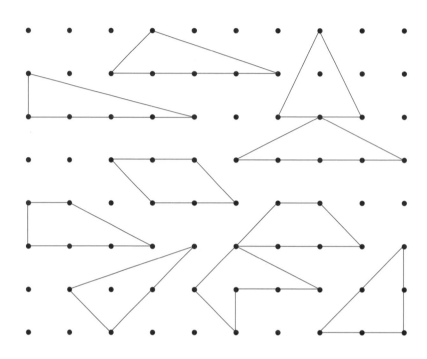

Create

Level A. Students may create problems involving other shapes on the dot paper, or they may extend the problem to squares on larger dot paper. Note that the number of triangles possible by connecting the dots is much greater than the number of squares possible. Even with only four dots, there are four triangles possible. With nine dots, there are 36 possible triangles. Exploring the total possible number of triangles or any other polygon for any given number of dots again encourages students to look for patterns, use charts or diagrams, make conjectures, and test hypotheses.

Level B. The Level B problems extend the Level A problems to a larger number of dots and ask students to find the area of the squares. Students might extend this by generalizing the possible number of squares to even greater numbers of dots or may ask other questions about areas. Students who construct a variety of ways to find areas of polygons can build a solid foundation for understanding formulas and other generalizations about areas of two-dimensional polygons and can build on this to understand surface area and volume of three-dimensional space figures.

Level C. In these problems, students continue to build on their concepts of area. Students might extend these problems to finding polygons with areas other than two square units or may expand to finding areas of polygons or other shapes that cannot be drawn on dot paper. Students may also continue to explore areas on dot paper or geoboards by searching for a relationship between the number of dots or pegs on the border and dots or pegs in the interior of a polygon and the area of that polygon. Pick's Theorem states that the area of any polygon that can be formed on a geoboard can be found by taking 1/2 of the number of pegs on the border, adding the number of pegs in the interior, and subtracting 1. Students who make a chart of the number of pegs on the border, the number of pegs in the interior, and the area of a polygon may discover this relationship for themselves. Others may wish to use the Internet or resource books to explore Pick's Theorem further.

Discussion

Geoboards offer the opportunity for a number of geometric explorations and can be purchased for only a few dollars. Many students will benefit from being able to manipulate the rubber bands on a geoboard before recording their solutions on the dot paper, making the geoboards well worth the purchase price. If you worry about students shooting rubber bands at each other while working on geoboards, you might initially give each student just one rubber band for the early investigations. Most students, however, become engrossed in the explorations, and shooting the rubber bands is not a problem.

There are numerous problem-solving books and Internet sites with further dot/geoboard problems. Encourage students to explore these and challenge each other with their findings.

Form 4.1. Framed—Level A

The Girls and Boys Club is designing tiled picture frames to sell at a local craft fair. They have priced the following frames based on the white tiles around the outside:

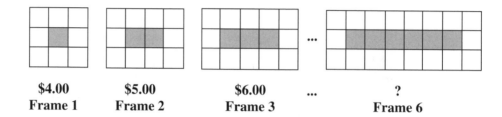

$4.00 $5.00 $6.00   ...   ?
Frame 1   Frame 2   Frame 3   Frame 6

- How many gray tiles are in Frame 6? How many white tiles are there around the outside of Frame 6?

- If the same pattern continues, how much should Frame 6 cost? Why?

- If the same pattern continues, how many gray tiles are in Frame 26? If the same pattern continues, how many white tiles are there around the outside of Frame 26?

- If the same pattern continues, how much should Frame 26 cost? Why?

- Describe the frame that they should sell for $18 and explain your reasoning.

- If N stands for the number of any frame, give a rule to explain how you might find the cost (C) using N. Explain your rule.

Compare your responses to those of a classmate. Did you get the same answers? Did you work the problems the same way?

Make up some frame questions of your own and challenge a classmate to solve them. Do you agree on the answer and the best method of solution?

Form 4.2.   Framed—Level B

The Girls and Boys Club is designing tiled picture frames to sell at a local craft fair. They have priced the following frames based on the white tiles around the edge of the frames:

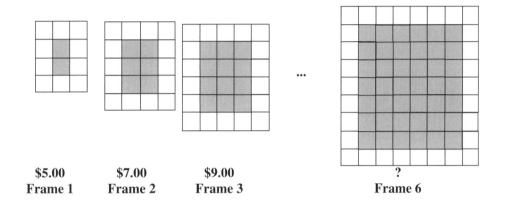

$5.00 $7.00 $9.00   ?
Frame 1   Frame 2   Frame 3   Frame 6

- How many white tiles are there around the outside of Frame 6? Frame 26? Frame N?

- If the same pattern continues, how much should Frame 6 cost? Why?

- If the same pattern continues, how much should Frame 26 cost? Why?

- Describe the frame that they should sell for $89 and explain your reasoning.

- If N stands for the number of any frame, give a rule to explain how you might find the cost (C) using N. Explain your rule.

Compare your responses to those of a classmate. Did you get the same answers? Did you work the problems the same way?

Make up some frame questions of your own and challenge a classmate to solve them. Do you agree on the answer and the best method of solution?

Form 4.3. Framed—Level C

The Art Club is designing tiled frames to sell at a local craft fair. They have priced the following frames based on the white tiles around the outside of the frames:

The white tiles that the students are buying cost 30¢ apiece and the other materials they are using for the frames have been donated and cost them nothing.

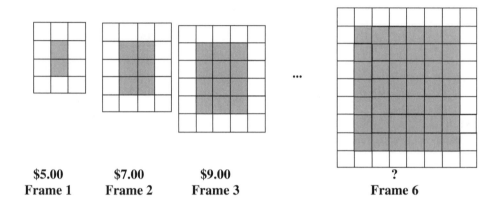

$5.00	$7.00	$9.00	?
Frame 1	**Frame 2**	**Frame 3**	**Frame 6**

- A frame has 12 gray tiles in the middle in a rectangular pattern, but it is not the same as Frame 3. Sketch what it might look like. How many white tiles might frame it? How much should it cost?

- How much profit can the club expect to make if they sell each of the four frames pictured above? Explain your reasoning.

- Describe the frame that they should sell for $195 and explain your reasoning.

- Describe the frame that should have a profit of $10 and explain your reasoning.

- If N stands for the number of any frame, give a rule to explain how you might find the profit (P) using N. Explain your rule.

Compare your responses to those of a classmate. Did you get the same answers? Did you work the problems the same way?

Make up some frame questions of your own and challenge a classmate to solve them. Do you agree on the answer and the best method of solution?

Form 4.4.   Shape Up—Level A

Trace the rectangle below and cut it out. Cut along the diagonal to make two congruent right triangles.

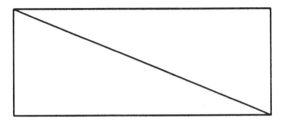

Join congruent sides of the two triangles together to form new polygons such as the one below.

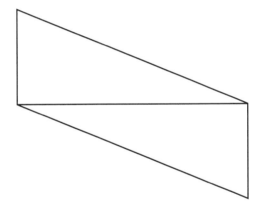

Trace around the outside of your new shape and give its geometric name or names. This shape is a quadrilateral because it has four sides, and it is a parallelogram because the opposite sides are parallel.

How many different shapes can you make? (Shapes are considered the same, or congruent, if you can turn or flip one shape to make it fit exactly on another shape.) Compare your results to those of a classmate. Did you both make the same shapes?

Start with a different polygon and cut it into two congruent pieces. How many shapes can you make from this?

Create your own Shape Up puzzles and trade with a classmate. Do you get the same answers?

Form 4.5. Shape Up—Level B

Trace the rectangle below and cut it out. Cut along the diagonal to make two congruent right triangles and a rectangle.

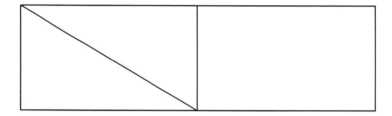

Join congruent sides of the two triangles or the rectangle together to form new polygons that include all three shapes such as the one below.

Trace around the outside of your new shape and give its geometric name or names. This shape is a quadrilateral because it has four sides, and it is a parallelogram because the opposite sides are parallel.

How many different shapes can you make? (Shapes are considered the same if you can turn or flip one shape to make it fit exactly on another shape.) Compare your results to those of a classmate. Did you both make the same shapes?

How do the areas of the new shapes compare to the original rectangle? How do the perimeters compare?

Create some Shape Up questions of your own and challenge a classmate to solve them. Do you agree on the answers and the best method of solution?

Form 4.6.   Shape Up—Level C

The following shapes are the seven puzzle pieces that make the famous Chinese tangram puzzles.

Trace these shapes and cut them out. Use these shapes to form other geometric shapes.

Try to make a square using two, three, four, five, six, or all seven pieces. Compare your results to your friends. Work together to see how many different squares you can make. Draw your results on a large poster to share with the class. If the entire square has a value of one square unit, what is the fractional value of the other pieces in each square?

What other geometric shapes can you make? How many tangram puzzle pieces did you use for each? For each figure, if the value of the entire figure is one square unit, what is the fractional value of each of the other pieces?

Research the history of tangrams using the Internet or the library. Find or design puzzles using all seven of the pieces, and trade with a friend.

Form 4.7. Connect the Dots—Level A

Connect the dots below to make squares. How many squares can you make with corners on the dots? _____

Hint: There are more than five squares. Don't forget that squares are not always drawn with sides parallel to the edges of the paper. They do always have four right angles, though.

```
•    •    •

•    •    •

•    •    •
```

Predict the number of squares that you can make connecting the dots below. _____

Draw all the possible squares you can by connecting the dots. Was your prediction correct? _____ Did you find more than 14 squares? _____

```
•    •    •    •

•    •    •    •

•    •    •    •

•    •    •    •
```

Make up your own Connect the Dots problems and trade with a class-mate. Did you get the same answers?

Form 4.8. Connect the Dots—Level B

Connect the dots below to make squares. How many squares can you make with corners on the dots? _____

Hint: There are more than 30 squares. Don't forget that squares are not always drawn with sides parallel to the edges of the paper. They do always have four right angles, though.

.   .   .   .   .

.   .   .   .   .

.   .   .   .   .

.   .   .   .   .

.   .   .   .   .

Sketch all the squares that you find on the dots above. Find the area of each of the squares. What is the area of the following square? How do you know?

Complete the chart below to record the squares you have found. Record the number of squares with each of the following areas:

Area (in square units)	Number of Squares
1	16
2	
4	
5	
8	
9	
10	
16	1

Make up your own Connect the Dots problems and trade with a classmate. Did you get the same answers?

Form 4.9. Connect the Dots—Level C

The following polygons have an area of two square units.

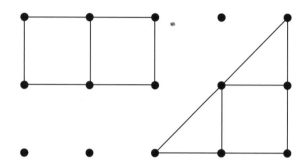

Make as many different polygons as possible that have an area of two square units. Use drawings and/or area formulas to convince a classmate that each of your figures has an area of two square units. Try to find at least 10 different (not congruent) shapes.

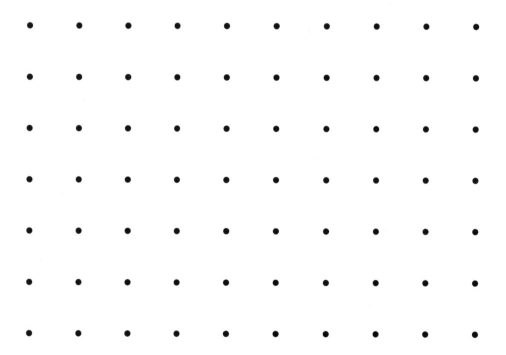

Compare the shapes you have found to those of several of your classmates. How many different shapes can you find together?

Make up your own Connect the Dots problems and trade with a classmate. Did you get the same answers?

Data Analysis and Probability 5

Investigations in this chapter will focus on developing a student's sense of data analysis and probability concepts such as formulating questions, making predictions, understanding basic probability, and collecting, organizing, analyzing, and displaying data.

In all explorations, students are asked to make conjectures and test their hypotheses using a variety of strategies. Activities again make use of the heuristic and questioning strategies outlined in Chapter 1, and teachers and students are encouraged to build upon the investigations and each other's reasoning with other questions and explorations of their own.

All the investigations in Chapter 5 are related to the NCTM Data Analysis and Probability Standards:

Instructional programs from prekindergarten through grade 12 should enable all students to

Formulate questions that can be addressed with data and collect, organize, and display relevant data to answer them

Select and use appropriate statistical methods to analyze data

Develop and evaluate inferences and predications that are based on data

Understand and apply basic concepts of probability (NCTM, 2000, p. 400)

Be sure to work and reflect on the problems on the reproducible forms yourself before reading about the solutions. In that way, you will reach a much deeper understanding of the mathematics involved before giving the problems to the students to think about. It is most helpful if you can get a group of teachers to solve these problems together before introducing them to the students. You might brainstorm a list of questions that will help students think more deeply about the mathematical concepts they are developing.

INVESTIGATION ONE: WHO'S GOT THE BUTTON?

Relate

NCTM Principles and Standards

- Sort and classify objects according to their attributes
- Organize data about objects
- Use counting techniques for simple compound events, using such methods as organized lists and tree diagrams
- Propose and justify conclusions and predictions based on data
- Use conjectures to formulate new questions

Prior Mathematical Concepts

- Recognize likenesses and differences
- Distinguish shapes, sizes, and colors

Typical Textbook Exercises

- Circle the object that is larger
- Put these in order from the largest to the smallest

Investigate

These investigations ask students to organize data according to multiple attributes. Students must be able to classify, organize, and create data using at least three different characteristics simultaneously. Students are encouraged to use a number of different organization schemes in solving these problems and in creating new ones.

Young children may wish to read "The Lost Button" from *Frog and Toad Are Friends* by Arnold Lobel (1979) and discuss all the different types of buttons that were found in the story before they begin this investigation.

Level A—See Form 5.1 on page 123

Level A, Form 5.1. In this investigation, students are asked to determine the number of different buttons that are possible using four different colors, three different sizes, and two different

Illustration 5.1. Student Solution to Who's Got the Button? Activity

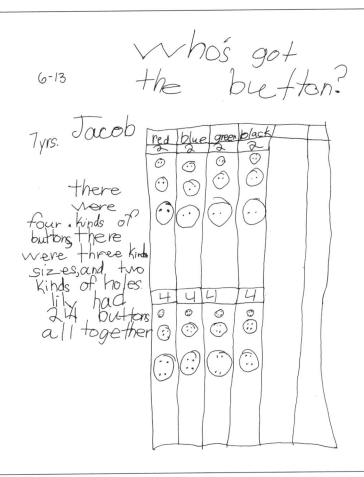

numbers of holes. To do this, students must be able to organize information to ensure that they determine all possible combinations and that they do not repeat any possible combinations of characteristics. Students who just start drawing buttons may find that they have repeated some combinations of attributes while leaving others out. They should be encouraged to organize their information and list all the possibilities before beginning to draw.

Many students will decide to first list all the possibilities for one color and then will list those same combinations in each of the other colors. For example, a student may list the green buttons as green large two holes, green medium two holes, green small two holes, green large four holes, green medium four holes, and green small four holes and then announce that she knows that there are 24 buttons in Lily's set because there are six green buttons and there must then be six red buttons, six black buttons, and six blue buttons.

Level B—See Form 5.2 on page 124

Level B, Form 5.2. This game involves the use of a Venn diagram, which is named after John Venn, a British mathematician who was famous for his work with mathematical logic and diagrams to represent the union and intersection of sets.

In this game, students must first choose two attributes of a button such as color and size as labels for the two loops. If the children choose two attributes from the same category such as two colors or two different numbers of holes, there will be no buttons in the intersection. Students on the other team must deduce the labels for the loops from the given clues. Note that determining that a given button does not belong in either of the two loops and must go on the outside of the circles gives students as much or more information about the labels for the loops as does putting the button in the correct section inside the loops.

Level C—See Form 5.3 on page 125

Level C, Form 5.3. The investigation from Level B is extended to three loops. This is considerably more difficult than the investigation with two loops and may need more adult supervision when students first play to ensure that the correct

Figure 5.1.

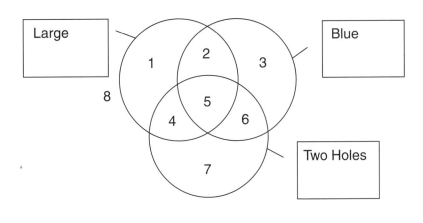

information is given as to whether or not a button belongs in a certain area. For example in Figure 5.1, note that there are eight areas numbered 1 to 8.

The buttons in Section 1 are large with four holes and not blue. In Section 2, they are large and blue and have four holes. In section 3, the buttons are blue with four holes and not large. In Section 4, they are large with two holes and not blue. In Section 5, all three attributes come together for large blue buttons with two holes. In Section 6, the buttons are blue with two holes and not large, and buttons in Section 7 have two holes, are not large and not blue. In Section 8, the buttons have four holes, are not large and are not blue. Note that the characteristics that buttons are not are just as important in locating the buttons as the things that they are.

Evaluate and Communicate

Level A. As the students determine the buttons, they will probably use a variety of techniques. Some children may lay out the four colors that they will need to color the buttons and then begin with listing or coloring the six buttons of one color. Others may first draw all the large buttons with two holes (one of each color) and then draw the large buttons with four holes before moving to the medium buttons and the small buttons.

Students who use different techniques should compare methods and reasoning to determine if they have each listed the same 24 buttons. Some students may list buttons in columns according to their colors, as shown in Table 5.1.

TABLE 5.1

Blue	Black	Green	Red
Large, 2 hole	Large, 2 hole	Large, 2 hole	Large, 2 hole
Large, 4 hole	Large, 4 hole	Large, 4 hole	Large, 4 hole
Medium, 2 hole	Medium, 2 hole	Medium, 2 hole	Medium, 2 hole
Medium, 4 hole	Medium, 4 hole	Medium, 4 hole	Medium, 4 hole
Small, 2 hole	Small, 2 hole	Small, 2 hole	Small, 2 hole
Small, 4 hole	Small, 4 hole	Small, 4 hole	Small, 4 hole

This type of listing is sometimes called a Carroll diagram because it was frequently used by Lewis Carroll (Charles Dodgson), the author of *Alice's Adventures in Wonderland*, who was also a British mathematician who did his work in the area of mathematical logic around the same time as John Venn.

Other students may use a tree diagram to sort all the buttons such as the one shown in Figure 5.2.

Figure 5.2.

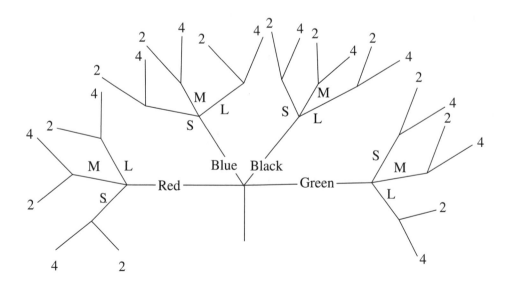

Illustration 5.2. Another Student Solution to Who's Got the Button? Activity

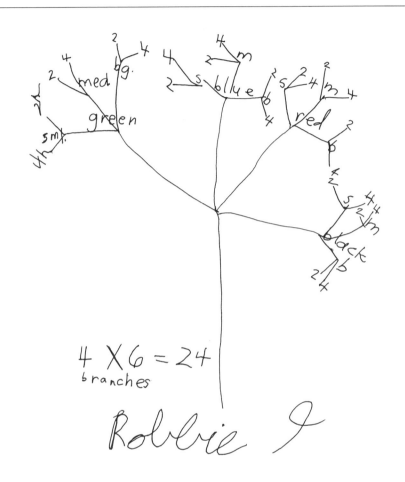

Encourage students to develop their own methods of organizing information and compare them. Some students will prefer using tree diagrams, others Carroll diagrams, and still other students will prefer their own invented methods of organization.

Level B. It is good to play the Venn diagram game with teams of two or three students playing against each other rather than individuals so students can discuss their strategies with each other. It is easy to give wrong answers or to become confused when placing buttons in different sections. Discussions with a partner help to avoid some of these mistakes.

Level C. With three loops rather than two, it becomes even more critical to discuss strategies and responses with a partner. Students might want to label the sections on the playing surface as well as on their paper with the numbers 1 to 8 to help them avoid making any mistakes in giving or asking for clues.

Create

Level A. Students who have found that there are 24 buttons in Lily's set may want to create other sets of attribute materials to describe other events that they have read about or to use for holidays and seasons such as fall leaves, spring flowers, or Halloween pumpkins. For example, students might wish to find all the jack-o'-lanterns they can make with two different sizes, three types of eyes, and two types of noses ($2 \times 3 \times 2$ or 12), or the number of different spring flowers with three types of flowers, two colors, and three different numbers of leaves ($3 \times 2 \times 3$ or 18). Students who have created a number of different sets should realize that they could determine the total number of pieces in a set by multiplying together the number of attributes in each category. For example, a set of attribute materials made of three colors, four sizes, and five shapes would have $3 \times 4 \times 5$ or 60 elements or pieces in it. Students can create a number of attribute games using these pieces. They may also enjoy games sold commercially such as Set, in which players try to match a number of attributes on cards from a deck of cards with different shapes, colors, and numbers.

Level B. Students might create other games using the two-loop Venn diagram with the button pieces that they have created or using other sets of attribute materials, including commercial attribute materials with pieces of different shapes, or other attribute sets that they have created for the Level A investigation. For example, one team of students might decide on secret rules for the two loops and then place six to eight buttons in the loops in the correct location with one button incorrectly placed. The other team would then have to guess which button is in the incorrect place and move that button to the correct location. Games that students create might be left in a learning center for other students to play during free time.

Level C. Games created for the three-loop Venn diagram can be challenging for students at all levels. Students who have mastered the two-loop games might be challenged to create and play games with three loops. Note that some students will want to create labels for the games that involve the negation of attributes, such as all the buttons that are not black belong in one loop and buttons that are not small in another. These games can become quite challenging and help students develop their logical reasoning as well as their abilities to sort and organize information.

Discussion

The investigations in this section are designed to enhance higher-level thinking as well as data analysis capabilities. They build upon some of the work of two famous mathematicians, John Venn and Lewis Carroll, who did much of their research and writing in the field of mathematical logic. Students may wish to investigate some of their work using the Internet or the library to find other games, problems, puzzles, and activities that build upon this work with sets, attributes, and logic.

INVESTIGATION TWO: ON YOUR MARK

Relate

NCTM Principles and Standards

- Predict the probability of outcomes of simple experiments and test the predictions
- Use proportionality and a basic understanding of probability to make and test conjectures about the results of experiments and simulations
- Compute probabilities for simple compound events, using such methods as organized lists and tree diagrams

Prior Mathematical Concepts

- Distinguish between even and odd numbers
- Add one-digit numbers
- Record data on charts and tables

Typical Textbook Exercises

- Circle all the even numbers: 2, 3, 4, 5, 6
- Fill in the blanks: 3 + 4 = _____   6 + 2 = _____

Investigate

In these activities, students begin to explore simple probability concepts using spinners and dice to generate random numbers. They will compare experimental probability to mathematical probability by actually playing the race games (experimental probability) and then comparing the results of the actual games to the mathematical probability that they calculate by completing a chart or tree diagram or making an organized list. In this way, the students build upon the organized lists and charts that they have developed in the Buttons investigations. Investigations in this section build from one using a simple three-section spinner that generates 9 ordered pairs to those using two dice that generate 36 ordered pairs.

Level A, Form 5.4. In playing this game, if you have clear, blank spinners, students can place one directly on top of the reproducible form and spin. If you do not have clear spinners, you may make a copy of the master and mount it on poster board. Bend one part of a paper clip straight up and poke it through the center of the spinner from the back. Tape the rest of the paper clip to the back of the master. Use another paper clip as the spinner by putting it over the part of the first spinner that is sticking up.

Level A—See Form 5.4 on page 126

Ask students to predict whether they think that Even Steven or Odd Otto will win more often when playing with the given spinner before they actually have a chance to play the game. Many students will think that because the spinner has two odd numbers and only one even number, the odd numbers will win more often. As they play the game a few times, they might note that this is not generally the case. Ask students to discuss their results of actually playing the game and compare this to their predictions. Discuss the results as a whole class to determine if results from individual games were typical of other players.

Level B—See Form 5.5 on page 127

Level B, Form 5.5. Before playing the games with the dice, students should play the Level A game with the spinner and analyze the results. Ask the students to predict the results of this game before playing. This time, each die has the same number of even and odd numbers, so students may predict that the multiplication game will be a fair game. Again, as they play, they will probably realize that when multiplying, Even Steven wins the game more often. Direct the students to analyze why they think this is the case. Again, compare the results from individual games to those obtained by the entire class.

Repeat the predictions before playing the addition game with the dice. Will adding rather than multiplying have an effect on the results? Why or why not? Allow the students to play the game and compile their results as a whole class. Why are these results different from the product game?

Level C—See Form 5.6 on page 128

Level C, Form 5.6. Level C of On Your Mark asks students to predict whether certain sums will appear more often than others. Students who have played the Level A and Level B versions of On Your Mark have analyzed results for even and odd but may not have thought about how often actual sums occur. They may think that the player who chooses Outer Space is much more likely to win, because that player has many more numbers to choose from. They may be surprised to find that it is actually more likely that the Inner Space player will win in spite of having fewer numbers. After students have played the game with a partner, they should discuss the results in small groups and then in a whole class to determine if their results were unusual or common.

Evaluate and Communicate

Level A. After students have had an opportunity to play the game a few times and to compare their results to others in the class, ask them to make a list of all the possible outcomes of spinning two spinners and adding the results. Students who have completed the Who's Got the Button? investigation should have a variety of ways to list the results. They may list ordered pairs or use a tree or Carroll diagram to make sure that they have found all the possible combinations. The following are a few of the possible methods they might use for this analysis.

Ordered pairs: (1,1—even; 1,2—odd; 1,3—even; 2,1—odd, 2,2—even; 2,3—odd, 3,1—even; 3,2—odd; 3,3—even)

Figure 5.3. Carroll Diagram

	1	2	3
1	Even	Odd	Even
2	Odd	Even	Odd
3	Even	Odd	Even

Figure 5.4. Tree Diagram

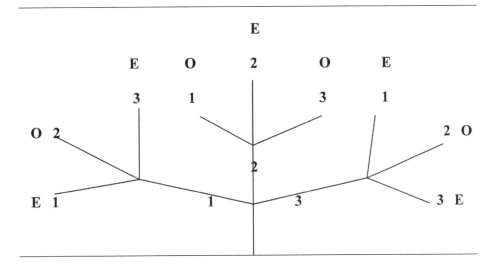

Allow time for students to share the various methods that they have used to determine all the possible combinations of numbers from spinning both spinners. Note that each method shows that mathematically you can expect to get five even sums for every four odd sums. This would suggest that the player who has chosen Even Steven should win more often than the player with Odd Otto. Compare these results from determining mathematical probability to those obtained experimentally from actually playing the game. Generally, the more games that are played, the closer the experimental results should be to the mathematical probability.

Level B. Students who have determined the mathematical probability from Level A of this game should be able to extend one or more of those methods to determine the mathematical probability using dice.

Ordered Pairs for Multiplication Game

1,1—O; 1,2—E; 1,3—O; 1,4—E; 1,5—O; 1,6—E

2,1—E; 2,2—E; 2,3—E; 2,4—E; 2, 5—E; 2,6—E

3,1—O; 3,2—E; 3,3—O; 3,4—E; 3,5—O; 3,6—E

4,1—E; 4,2—E; 4,3—E; 4,4—E; 4, 5—E; 4,6—E

5,1—O; 5,2—E; 5,3—O; 5,4—E; 5,5—O; 5,6—E

6,1—E; 6,2—E; 6,3—E; 6,4—E; 6, 5—E; 6,6—E

Figure 5.5. Carroll Diagram for Multiplication Game

	1	2	3	4	5	6
1	O	E	O	E	O	E
2	E	E	E	E	E	E
3	O	E	O	E	O	E
4	E	E	E	E	E	E
5	O	E	O	E	O	E
6	E	E	E	E	E	E

Tree Diagram. Other students may make a tree diagram with six branches at the bottom and six branches coming out of each of those to determine the same 36 combinations of numbers.

Note that whichever method the students choose to use, the mathematical results of 27 even products and only 9 odd products are the same. Students should discuss why this is the case and whether this matches their experimental results from actually playing the game. Note that this game heavily favors even products, so it is likely that the Even Steven player will beat the Odd Otto player nearly all the time.

After determining the mathematical probability from the multiplication game and comparing that to the experimental results, ask the students to predict what the mathematical probability will be for the addition game. Students who have played this game first and analyzed the experimental results may realize that the Odd Otto player wins about the same number of times as the Even Steven player.

Encourage students to determine the possible mathematical combinations from adding the two numbers shown on the dice. Note that students should find that there are 18 even sums and 18 odd sums. This is a "fair game." That means that the player who chooses Even Steven has exactly the same chances of winning as the player who chooses Odd Otto. Students should discuss why this is different from the results from the multiplication game.

Level C. Students who have analyzed experimental results may realize that the Inner Space player has won more often, but may not realize why this is the case. Again, ask the students to determine the mathematical probability for each sum using any method. A Carroll diagram gives the following sums in Figure 5.6.

Figure 5.6. Carroll Diagram for On Your Mark—Level C

	1	2	3	4	5	6
1	2	3	4	5	6	7
2	3	4	5	6	7	8
3	4	5	6	7	8	9
4	5	6	7	8	9	10
5	6	7	8	9	10	11
6	7	8	9	10	11	12

Ask the students why the Inner Space player has won more often. Students might use a number of different methods to analyze the results. For example, a student might make a chart like the one in Figure 5.7.

Figure 5.7. Chart for On Your Mark—Level C

Sum	2	3	4	5	6	7	8	9	10	11	12
Number of times sum appears	1	2	3	4	5	6	5	4	3	2	1

Note that the Inner Space player has numbers (5, 6, 7, and 8) that will appear on average 20 times out of 36 rolls, and the Outer Space player has numbers that will appear on average 16 times out of 36 rolls. Even though the Outer Space player has more numbers, they do not occur as often as the "inner" numbers. Because the probabilities are not equal, the game is not a fair game.

Create

Level A. After students have had a chance to play the game and analyze the experimental and mathematical results, they should create other games of their own. They may wish to redesign the spinner to make this a fair game. A spinner with the same number of even and odd numbers will be fair for addition but not for multiplication when playing even versus odd. Why?

Level B. Students who have analyzed the even and odd results for addition and multiplication for common six-sided dice may wish to play the game using other types of dice or other operations. Each time the students design a new game, ask them to predict the results, play the game to collect experimental data, analyze the mathematical probability, and compare the results.

Level C. After playing the Outer/Inner Space game, students should try to develop rules for a Moon Race that would be a fair game. There are numerous ways to do this, and students should play and analyze each other's games to determine experimentally as well as mathematically whether the games are truly fair. Note that experimental results do not always match the mathematical expectations. Students should discuss why this is so.

Discussion

Young children may not understand that mathematical probability should predict the experimental results. They may believe that wishing for a certain number will cause it to appear on the spinner, or that if a certain sum has not appeared for awhile on the dice, it is more likely to show up the next time because it is about time for that sum to occur. (This also seems to be believed by many adults as they play the lottery or gamble on slot machines.) Students may need to play the games many times, perhaps recurring over a period of years, to realize that just wishing for something does not make it happen.

INVESTIGATION THREE: BULL'S-EYE

Relate

NCTM Principles and Standards

- Find, use, and interpret measures of center and spread
- Understand what the mean does and does not indicate about the data set

- Propose and justify conclusions and predictions that are based on data

Prior Mathematical Concepts

- Add using any number of addends
- Divide using one-digit divisors
- Find the mean of a group of numbers

Typical Textbook Exercises

- What is the mean of the following list of numbers? 2, 5, 7, 9 12
- What is the sum of 5 + 12 + 15 + 24?

Investigate

These investigations involve finding the mean, but students have to think more deeply than typical mean problems. They must analyze a number of different possibilities for each problem and use that analysis to answer the questions. Some of the problems have more than one correct solution, and students must eliminate some choices to determine whether they have found every possibility.

Level A, Form 5.7. For the first investigation, students must realize that to get a mean of 7 after three throws, the total of the three throws must be 21. That means that every dart must have hit the dartboard, because you cannot get a total of 21 with only one or two addends. It is possible that they each had three 7s, but this is not the only solution. Students should organize their data in some fashion to determine if they have exhausted all the possibilities.

Level A—See Form 5.7 on page 129

Level B, Form 5.8. In this round, students should build upon their organization scheme from the first round to determine all the ways to get a total of 30 using fewer than seven addends. A chart or an organized list will probably be most useful, but students may do this in a number of different ways. Note that there is one possibility using two darts, but there are several ways to get this sum with either four or six darts. This sum is not possible with an odd number of darts. Encourage students to discuss why this is the case.

Level B—See Form 5.8 on page 131

Level C—See Form 5.9 on page 133

Level C, Form 5.9. For the Level C problems, students know the averages, but they are not told the number of rounds. This means that the total scored is not immediately obvious. Students might then believe that there must be a number of correct answers as there were for the Level B questions. Encourage them to try to get these averages with any number of addends.

Evaluate and Communicate

Level A. Once students realize that the total for the three rounds must be 21, they then should search to find different ways to get 21 with three addends. The most obvious might be $7 + 7 + 7$, but this is not the only possibility. They might have gotten two 5s and one 11 ($5 + 5 + 11 = 21$) or one 15, one 5, and one 1 ($15 + 5 + 1 = 21$). Even though they did not have to get the same number of points on each round, because the averages are the same, they do have to have the same totals.

Students should discuss their reasoning as they work on these problems and compare their responses to see if they agree on the answers. These problems help students realize that just getting one answer is not enough. There are frequently a variety of ways to answer or solve a problem.

Level B. In this problem, because the number of rounds is unknown, the average or mean score is also unknown. With only odd numbers on the dartboard, the number of rounds must be an even number (adding an odd number of odd digits would produce an odd sum), but it is unknown whether the number of rounds is two, four, or six. The players must have the same mean score, however, because they have the same total after the same number of throws.

It is unknown whether the two players have hit the same sections of the target. If the game lasted only two rounds, they must have both hit two 15s. If the game lasted four or six rounds, there are a number of possibilities as shown in Table 5.2.

If the game lasted two rounds, the mean score would be 15; at four rounds, the mean score is 7.5; and at 6 rounds, the mean score is 5. Students should compare answers to determine if they have found all possibilities. Students who use different methods of organization might have difficulty in following the reasoning of another student, but sharing methods and discussing solutions helps all students expand their thinking to include alternate possibilities.

Level C. The investigation in Level C asks students to delve more deeply into the idea of averages. In this problem, because Colleen has

TABLE 5.2

Number on Dartboard	1	5	7	11	15	Total No. of Darts Thrown
					2	2
	4			1	1	6
	1		2		1	4
	3	1	1		1	6
		3			1	4
	1		1	2		4
	3	1		2		6
		1	2	1		4
	2	2	1	1		6
	2		4			6

thrown first and they have never missed the dartboard, you can probably assume that Colleen has thrown one more time than Dan, because he hopes to tie her with the next throw. Older students who have been introduced to some algebra might represent the problem as $9x = 8(x-1) + 11$. X in this case represents the number of throws that Colleen has, with nine as the average number of points on each thrown. Dan has only thrown $x-1$ times, with an average of eight points per throw. He hopes to tie by getting 11 points on the next throw. Solving this equation for x gives a total of three rounds. That would mean that Colleen has gotten a total of 27 points in three rounds, which she might have done with a 5, a 7, and a 15. Dan would have a total of 16 points after two rounds, which he might have done with a 1 and a 15.

Some students might argue that Dan and Colleen have both thrown the same number of darts and therefore the equation should be $9x = 8x + 11$. Solving this for x gives you 11 rounds, with Dan's total being 88 after Round 11. Students should discuss their solutions with each other to determine if they agree that this problem might have more than one right answer.

Create

Level A. Students might make up their own dartboards for each other as they create new questions or make up new questions about the same dartboard. Questions do not have to focus on the mean. If you are studying measures of central tendency and spread, you might encourage questions that also ask about the median, mode, and range.

Level B. If students create questions allowing any number of rounds, students should realize that the number of rounds must be even and that the greatest number of darts thrown if they all hit the board must be 30 (hitting one each time). Students might explore whether all other even numbers up to 30 are a possibility. Again, encourage explorations on other dartboards using other measures of spread and central tendency.

Level C. Older students who are delving deeply into this problem might extend the questions to others that involve using algebra to answer statistical questions about other measures of spread and central tendency. This might even involve questions about standard deviation if students have been introduced to that concept.

Discussion

The use of the dartboard in these investigations allows students to think about the effects of a variety of addends on a specific measure of central tendency, the mean. Many students have learned that the mean is found by adding up a list of numbers and then dividing by the number of addends, but they have not really internalized the concept of a mean as an average of a set of data. These investigations help students strengthen this understanding. Encouraging students to ask their own questions about other measures such as the median, mode, and range encourages them to think more deeply about many basic statistical measures and how they interrelate.

Form 5.1. Who's Got the Button?—Level A

Lily has a very special bag of buttons. It has one button of each possible combination of color, number of holes, and size. All of Lily's buttons are round.

When Lily sorts her buttons, she makes three piles for size—one pile for small buttons, one pile for medium buttons, and one pile for large buttons. When she sorts her buttons for colors, she makes four piles of buttons—one pile for green, one pile for black, one pile for red, and one pile for blue. When she sorts her buttons for holes, she makes two piles—one pile for two holes and one pile for four holes.

Draw Lily's buttons below, drawing one button in each square. Make sure that no two buttons are alike.

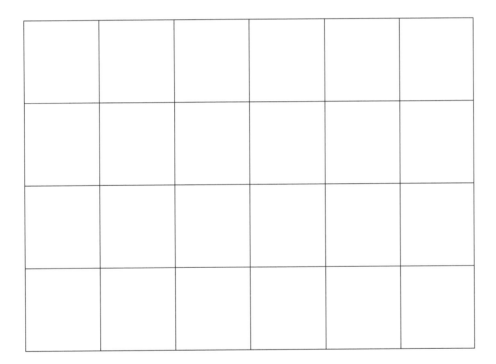

Cut out the squares and make up sorting questions about your buttons. Trade questions with a partner.

Form 5.2.   Who's Got the Button?—Level B

Decide on a rule for the loop labeled A and a different rule for the loop labeled B. (For example, you might choose a color for one loop and a size for the other.) Write these rules down and show your partner, but do not show the other team. What is the rule for the intersection of the two circles?

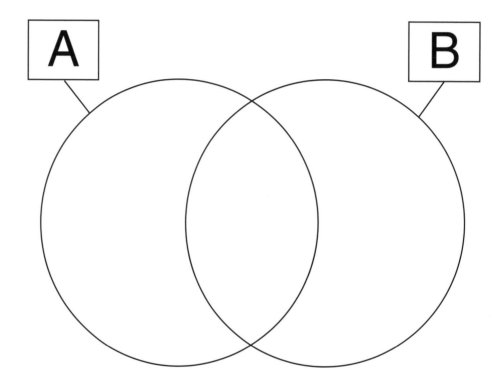

The other team will try to determine your rules by placing buttons in the loops. Each time the other team places a button in a section, tell them if the button is in the correct loop. If it is correct, the other team should leave the button where it is. If it is not correct, the other team should remove the button and guess again. When the other team thinks that they know your rules, they should ask, "Who's Got the Button?" They should then tell you the rule for Loop A and the rule for Loop B. If they are correct, it is the first team's turn to guess and the second team's turn to make up two new secret rules for Loops A and B.

Create your own games using the buttons and their attributes and play with a classmate.

Form 5.3.   Who's Got the Button?—Level C

Decide upon a rule for the loop labeled A, a different rule for the loop labeled B, and a third rule for loop C. (For example, you might choose a color for one loop, a size for the second loop, and a number of holes for the third.) Write these rules down and show your partner, but do not show the other team. What are the rules for the intersections of the circles?

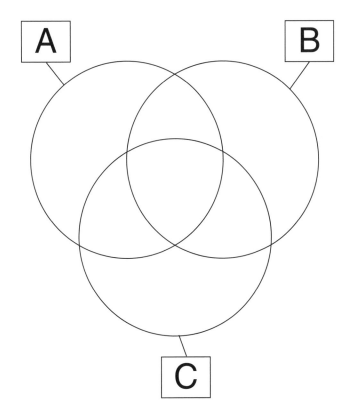

The other team will try to determine your rules by placing buttons in the loops. Each time the other team places a button in a section, tell them if the button is in the correct loop. If it is correct, the other team should leave the button where it is. If it is not correct, the other team should remove the button and guess again. When the other team thinks that they know your rules, they should ask, "Who's Got the Button?" They should then tell you the rule for each of the three loops. If they are correct, it is the first team's turn to guess and the second team's turn to make up new secret rules.

Create your own games using the buttons and their attributes and play with a classmate.

Form 5.4. On Your Mark—Level A

Even Steven and Odd Otto are planning a special kind of race. They will each spin the spinner below once and then add the two results together. If the sum is even, Even Steven will move his marker one space ahead. If the sum is odd, Odd Otto will move one space ahead. The first player to the finish line is the winner.

To determine who is Even Steven and who is Odd Otto, players should each spin the spinner once. The player with the smallest number may choose whether to be Steven or Otto. If there is a tie, players should spin again.

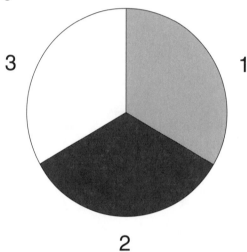

Even Steven Start										Finish
Odd Otto Start										Finish

Is this a fair game? Do both players have the same chance of winning?

Make up a new game for Even Steven and Odd Otto and play with a classmate. Is your game fair? Explain.

Form 5.5.   On Your Mark—Level B

Even Steven and Odd Otto are planning a special kind of race. They will each roll one die and then multiply the two numbers together. If the product is even, Even Steven will move his marker one space ahead. If the product is odd, Odd Otto will move one space ahead. The first player to the finish line is the winner.

To determine who is Even Steven and who is Odd Otto, players should each roll one die. The player with the smallest number may choose whether to be Steven or Otto. If there is a tie, players should roll again.

Even Steven Start									Finish
Odd Otto Start									Finish

Is this a fair game? Do both players have the same chance of winning? Explain.

Play the game by adding the two numbers together. Is the game fair now? Explain.

Make up a new game for Even Steven and Odd Otto and play with a classmate. Is your game fair? Explain.

Form 5.6. On Your Mark—Level C

Outer Space and Inner Space are racing to the moon. The game starts with a marker on each number. Markers for Outer Space (2, 3, 4, 9, 10, 11, and 12) should be one color, and the markers for Inner Space (5, 6, 7, and 8) should be a different color. Players each roll one die and add their values together. Players should move the marker ahead one space for the sum that is rolled. Outer Space moves ahead one space if the sum is 2, 3, 4, 9, 10, 11, or 12, and Inner Space moves ahead one space if the sum is 5, 6, 7, or 8.

To determine who goes first, the players should each roll one die. The player with the highest number should pick either Outer Space or Inner Space. The winner is the first player to reach the moon with any marker.

Moon

2							
3							
4							
5							
6							
7							
8							
9							
10							
11							
12							

Is this a fair game? Do both players have the same chance of winning? Explain your reasoning.

Make up a new race game and play with a classmate. Is your game fair? Explain.

Form 5.7. Bull's-Eye—Level A

Lindsey and Emma are playing darts on the board below. Each player throws one dart in each round. After three rounds, Lindsey and Emma each have scored an average of seven points.

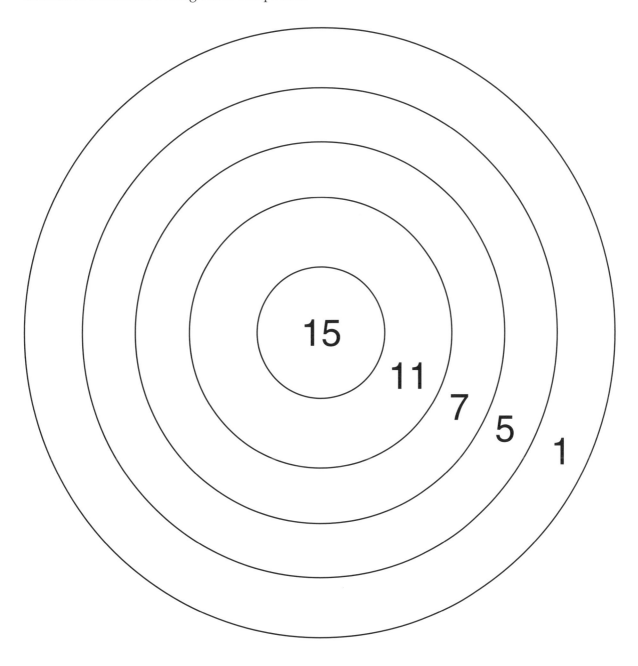

— ‖‖ ————————————

Form 5.7. (Continued)

Did either Lindsey or Emma miss the dartboard completely on any round? Explain.

Did Lindsey and Emma get the same number of points on each round? Explain.

Did Lindsey and Emma have the same totals after three rounds? Explain.

Make up your own questions about the dart game and trade with a classmate. Do you agree on the answers?

Form 5.8.   Bull's-Eye—Level B

Tyler and Chris are playing darts on the board below. Each player throws one dart in each round, and all darts hit the board. At the end of the game, Chris and Tyler are tied at a total of 30 points. The game lasted less than eight rounds.

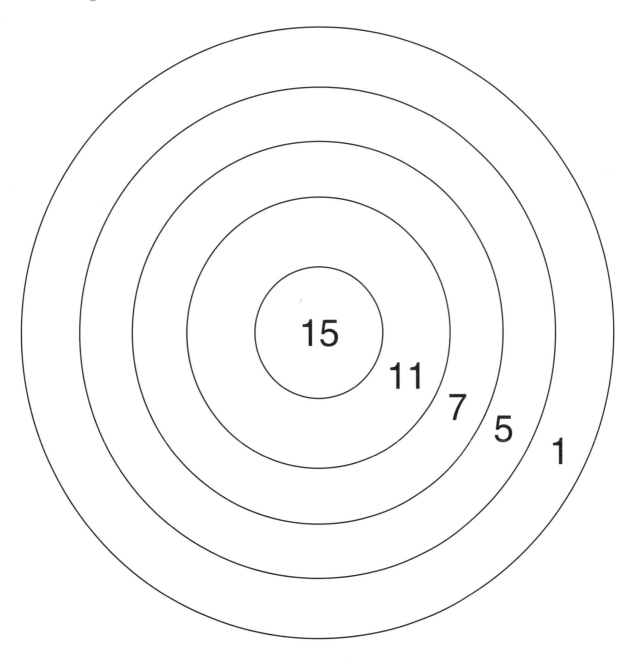

Do Chris and Tyler have the same mean score? What was the mean score? Explain.

Did Chris and Tyler hit the same sections of the target? Explain.

Is there more than one right answer to this problem? Explain.

Ask your own questions about the dart game and trade with a classmate. Compare your answers.

Form 5.9.   Bull's-Eye—Level C

Colleen and Dan are playing darts on the board below. Each player throws one dart in each round, and all darts hit the board. After playing for a while, Colleen, who threw first, says that she has an average of 9 points per throw. Dan's average is only 8 points per throw, but if he gets an 11 on his next throw, he will be tied with Colleen.

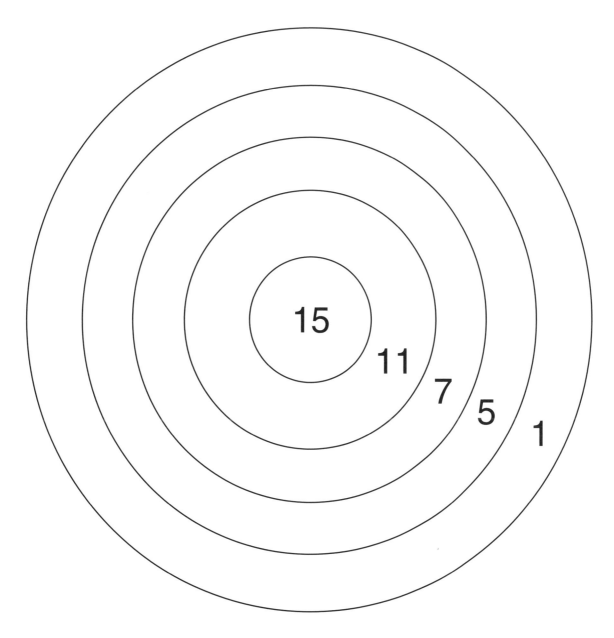

— ‖‖ ————————————

Form 5.8. (Continued)

How many darts has Colleen thrown?

What is Dan's total before the last throw? Explain.

Is there more than one right answer to this problem? Why or why not?

Make up your own target problems and trade with a classmate. Compare your solutions. Are any of the problems impossible to solve? Do any problems have more than one right answer?

Resources

If you have enjoyed the investigations in this book, you are probably wondering where you might find other similar resources to continue this type of problem solving. The resources listed here are designed to help you in this search. They are divided into sections for print references; commercial sources for problem-solving books, videos, software, calculators, and manipulatives; professional organizations for teachers of mathematically promising students; resources for curricula related to the NCTM *Principles and Standards*; interactive mathematics Web sites; Web sites with additional problems and investigations for teachers and students; mathematics competitions for students from K to 12; and summer and academic year programs for precollege students.

Wherever possible, I have included Internet sites where you can find more information from around the world. Please note that some of these sites change rapidly and may not be active, and other new sites with excellent resources are being created every day. I try to keep an updated list of some resources on my own Web site at www.nku.edu/~mathed. You might refer to this for more recent information.

PRINT RESOURCES

The following books and articles include some with more background on promising, gifted, and talented mathematics students and others with more ideas for encouraging students to think more deeply about mathematical ideas. I have given information on ordering these publications from Internet sites in parentheses where these are available.

Becker, Jerry, and Shimada, Shigeru (Eds.). (1997). *The open-ended approach: A new proposal for teaching mathematics*. Reston, VA: National Council of Teachers of Mathematics. (www.nctm.org)

Butterworth, Brian. (1997). *What counts: How every brain is hardwired for math*. New York: Free Press.

Cohen, Don. (1988). Variety of publications, including *Calculus by and for young people (ages 7, yes 7 and up)*. Champaign, IL: Don Cohen: The Mathman. (www.shout.net/~mathman/)

Dehaene, Stanislaus. (1997). *The number sense: How the mind creates mathematics*. New York: Oxford University Press.

Fielker, David. (1997). *Extending mathematical ability through whole class teaching*. London: Hodder & Stoughton.

Findell, Carol R., Gavin, M. Katherine, Greenes, Carole E., & Sheffield, Linda J. (2000). *Awesome math problems for creative thinking*. Chicago: Creative Publications. (www.wrightgroup.com/cgi-bin/catalog/series.cgi?series=00111)

House, Peggy A. (Ed.). (1987). *Providing opportunities for the mathematically gifted K–12*. Reston, VA: National Council of Teachers of Mathematics.

Koshy, Valsa. (2000). *Teaching mathematics to able children*. London: David Fulton.

National Council of Mathematics Teachers. (2001–). Navigations Series. (Series of PreK–12 books for teachers to support the NCTM Principles and Standards.) Reston, VA: Author. (www.nctm.org)

Ross, Patricia O. (1993). *National excellence: A case for developing America's talent*. Washington, DC: Office of Educational Research and Improvement. (www.ed.gov/pubs/DevTalent/toc.html)

Sheffield, Linda J. (1994). *Gifted and talented mathematics students and the curriculum and evaluation standards for school mathematics from the National Council of Teachers of Mathematics*. Commissioned by the National Research Council for Gifted Education, University of Connecticut, Jacob Javits Grant, U.S. Department of Education. (www.gifted. uconn.edu/resource.html#9404)

Sheffield, Linda J. (May 1997). Editorial: On my mind: From Doogie Howser to Dweebs? or How we went in search of Bobby Fischer and found that we are dumb and dumber. *Mathematics Teaching in the Middle School*, 2(6), 376-379.

Sheffield, Linda J. (November 1998). Tracks to success. *NCTM Dialogues*, 2(1), 3, 5. Available online at www.hctm.org/dialogues/1998=11.pdf

Sheffield, Linda J. (Ed.). (1999). *Developing mathematically promising students*. Reston, VA: National Council of Teachers of Mathematics. (www.nctm.org/)

Sheffield, Linda J. (Ed.). (October 1999). *Research and guidelines for nurturing gifted and talented students in mathematics and science*. School Science and Mathematics Association Leadership Benchmark Series. (www.ssma.org/monographs.html)

Sheffield, Linda J., Bennett, Jennie, Berriozábal, Manuel, DeArmond, Margaret, & Wertheimer, Richard. (December 1995). *Report of the task force on the mathematically promising*. NCTM News Bulletin, vol. 32.

Reston, VA: National Council of Mathematics Teachers. (www. tenet.edu/teks/math/mathforall/nctmpromising.html)

Sheffield, Linda J., & Cruikshank, Douglas E. (2000). *Teaching and learning elementary and middle school mathematics.* New York: Wiley.

COMMERCIAL EDUCATIONAL RESOURCES FOR MATHEMATICAL EXPLORATIONS

The following list includes a number of Web sites where you can find books, videos, calculators, software, games, and manipulative materials for mathematical explorations.

- AIMS sells products for integrating math and science curricula: www.aimsedu.org

- Annenberg/CPB publishes many educational videos and books for all grade levels: www.learner.org

- CCV Software sells a range of educational software: www.ccvsoftware.com

- Classroom Connect publishes guides to incorporating the Internet into classrooms: www.classroom.com

- Corwin Press publishes books on K – 12 education with many for educators of the gifted: www.corwinpress.com/

- D&H Education sells calculators and calculator accessories: www.buycalcs.com

- Delta Education sells a number of math manipulatives: www.delta-education.com

- Didax sells a wide range of curriculum materials for kindergarten through 12th grade: www.didaxinc.com

- EAI Education sells manipulatives and books: www.eaieducation.com

- Educational Resources sells educational software and hardware accessories: www.educationalresources.com

- ETA Cuisenaire produces books and manipulatives: www.etacuisenaire.com

- GPN sells videos and software: gpn.unl.edu

- Heinemann publishes several books for math educators: www.heinemann.com

- Learning Services sells educational software: www.learningservicesinc.com

- The Math Learning Center produces publications and manipulatives in line with the NCTM standards: www.mathlearningcenter.org

- Mathematics Pentathlon produces a program of problem-solving games and activities for use in Grades K–7: www.mathpentath.com

- MindWare sells toys for all ages designed to make learning fun: www.mindwareonline.com

- Nasco sells a variety of manipulatives: www.enasco.com

- National Council of Teachers of Mathematics has several books, journals, and electronic resources for parents and teachers: www.nctm.org

- PBS Video publishes videos on all topics, including elementary education: www.shoppbs.com/teachers

- Prufrock Press publishes books on gifted education: www.prufrock.com

- Riverdeep/The Learning Company is a leading producer of educational software: www.riverdeep.net

- Scholastic Publishing publishes children's books on virtually all topics: www.scholastic.com

- Science, Math & Gifted Products Catalog sells a variety of books, games and puzzles: www.smgproducts.com

- Software Express sells educational software: www.swexpress.com

- Summit Learning sells a variety of math and education related products: www.summitlearning.com

- Texas Instruments sells a variety of products for integrating technology into the classroom (e.g., calculators): education.ti.com

- Tom Snyder Productions develops software for use in classrooms: www.tomsnyder.com

- The Touchstones Discussion Project publishes a variety of textbooks that use a teaching approach designed to foster participation from all students: www.touchstones.org

- Valiant Technology USA produces the Math-U, portable machines that teach math curriculum through several activities, as well as the Roamer, a robot programmed in the LOGO language for K–8 students: www.valiant-technology.com/us

- The WEEA Equity Resource Center publishes many works on fostering gender equity in the classroom: www.edc.org/publications

PROFESSIONAL ORGANIZATIONS

The following are Web sites for professional organizations with resources for teachers at all grade levels. Many of these have valuable links to a wide variety of resources for parents and teachers of students of all ages.

- American Association for the Advancement of Science: www.aaas.org

- Council for Exceptional Children: www.cec.sped.org

- Mathematics Association of America: www.maa.org

- National Association for Gifted Children: www.nagc.org

- National Council of Supervisors of Mathematics: www.ncsmonline.org

- National Council of Teachers of Mathematics: www.nctm.org

- Research Council of Mathematics Learning: www.unlv.edu/ RCML

- School Science & Math Association: www.ssma.org

RESOURCES FOR CURRICULAR MATERIALS

The following are resources for mathematics curricula that have been developed to support the National Council of Teachers of Mathematics Principles and Standards. These include sites with information about the curricula as well as national evaluations of these materials.

- Eisenhower National Clearinghouse (ENC) (preschool–college): www.enc.org

- Exemplary and Promising Mathematics and Science Programs and Supporting Materials: www.enc.org/ professional/federalresources/exemplary

- Mathematically Sane (Teachers K–College): www.mathematicallysane.com/

- National Mathematics Resource Centers
    - K–12 Mathematics Curriculum Center (MCC): www.edc.org/mcc
    - Elementary: Alternatives for Rebuilding Curriculum (ARC) Center: www.comap.com/elementary/projects/arc
    - Middle School: The Show-Me Center: www.showmecenter.missouri.edu//Showme/default.html

– High School: Curricular Options in Mathematics for All
Secondary Students (COMPASS): www.ithaca.edu/compass

The *Exemplary and Promising Mathematics Programs Report* provides a
comprehensive description of each program designated by the Mathematics and Science Expert Panel as "exemplary" or "promising." Each
description includes a general overview, a discussion of related professional development, program costs, a description of program quality, evi-
dence of the program's effectiveness and success, the program's
educational significance and usefulness to others, and ordering and con-
tact information. This report cam be found at www.enc.org/professional/
federalresources/exemplary/promising/document.shtm?input=CDS-
000496-496_toc

Project 2061 is the long-term initiative of the American Association for
the Advancement of Science (AASP) working to reform K–12 science,
mathematics, and technology education nationwide. They have recently
released *Middle Grades Mathematics Textbooks: A Benchmarks-Based Evaluation* that can be found at www.project2061.org/matheval.

INTERACTIVE MATHEMATICS WEB SITES, APPLETS, AND VIRTUAL MANIPULATIVES

The following sites include a variety of interactive applets that give students the opportunity to manipulate virtual models that in many cases are
very similar to the concrete materials such as tangrams and geoboards
that many teachers use to support their mathematics curricula.

- Autograph: dynamic PC software for teaching calculus,
  coordinate geometry, statistics, and probability: www.autograph-
  math.com

- Dr. Super's Virtual and Concrete Math Manipulatives (Grades 3
  and up): www.galaxy.gmu.edu/~drsuper

- Educational Java Programs (Elementary–HS): arcytech.org/java

- ExploreMath.com (Middle School and up):
  www.exploremath.com/index.cfm

- Manipula Math with JAVA (Middle School and up):
  www.ies.co.jp/math/java/index.html

- National Library of Virtual Manipulatives for Interactive
  Mathematics (PreK–12, listed according to NCTM Principles and
  Standards categories): matti.usu.edu/nlvm/nav/vlibrary.html

- National Council of Teachers of Mathematics Illuminations i-
  Math Investigations (PreK–12): www.illuminations.nctm.org/
  imath/index.html

- SimCalc (Middle and High School):
  www.simcalc.umassd.edu

- Varnelle Moore's Primary Math Activities (PreK–2):
  mathforum.org/varnelle/index.html

OPEN-ENDED PROBLEMS—RESOURCES FOR TEACHERS

The following are a number of resources for teachers in locating other open-ended problems.

- Franklin Institute of Science Open-Ended Problems (Middle School): sln.fi.edu/school/math2

- Oregon Department of Education Assessment and Evaluation Samples of Open-Ended Math Tasks (Elementary–HS): www.col-ed.org/smcnws/elementary.html

- Performance Assessment Task Samples International (K–12): www.col-ed.org/smcnws/assesstask.html

- Ron Pelfrey's Open-Ended Mathematics Questions (Grade 4–HS): ftp://www.uky.edu/pub/arsi/openresponsequestions/mathorq.pdf

- Potent Problems (ages 6–adult): www.edmath.org/potent

- Southwest Missouri State University's Problem Corner (HS and up): math.smsu.edu/~les/POTW.html

- Akihiko Takahashi Open-Ended Problem Solving on the Web (all ages): www.mste.uiuc.edu/users/aki/open_ended

- TIMSS Online Challenge (Elementary–HS): timssonline.cse.ucla.edu/index01.htm or www.getsmarter.org

Problems and Resources for Students

There are lots of great problems for students to explore on the following sites.

- 4000 Years of Women in Science: crux.astr.ua.edu/4000WS/4000WS.html

- AIMS puzzle page (Grades K–9): www.aimsedu.org/Puzzle/PuzzleList.html

- Aunty Math: Math Challenges for K–5 Learners: www.auntymath.com

- Cool Math (ages 13–adult): www.coolmath.com

- Cool Math 4 Kids (Preschool–HS): www.coolmath4kids.com

- Family Math (K–12): equals.lhs.berkeley.edu

- Figure This: Math Challenges for Families: www.figurethis.org/index40.htm

- Funbrain (Preschool–Adult): www.funbrain.com

- Get Smarter (Take the TIMSS Challenge: Grades 3–HS): www.getsmarter.org

- Gifted Resources Home Page (all ages): www.eskimo.com/~user/kids.html

- Interactive Mathematics Miscellany and Puzzles (K–12): www.cut-the-knot.com/content.html

- Institute for Mathematics and Computer Science (IMACS): www.imacs.org

  - Online Curricula Division (HS and up): www.eimacs.org

  - Enrichment Program (Grades K–8): www.imacs.org/imacs_site/envapmathenrichment.asp

- The Jason Project (Middle School math, science, and technology): www.jasonproject.org

- Making Mathematics: Mentored Research Projects for Young Mathematicians (Grades 7–12): www2.edc.org/makingmath

- Math Brain Teasers (Grades 3–8): www.eduplace.com/math/brain

- Math Forum (K–12): mathforum.org

  - Ask Dr. Math from Forum (K–College): mathforum.org/dr.math

  - Problems of the Week: mathforum.org/pow

  - K–12 Math Problems, Puzzles, Tips & Tricks: mathforum.org/k12/mathtips

  - Math Ideas for Science Fair Projects: mathforum.org/teachers/mathproject.html

  - ESCOT PoW Archives: mathforum.org/escotpow

  - Internet Mathematics Library: mathforum.org/library

- Math Projects for Science Fairs (Elementary–HS): camel.math.ca/Education/mpsf

- Mathematics Problems for Japanese Sixth Graders: www.japanese-online.com/math/index.htm

- Mathematics Problems of the Week Contest Page (Elementary–HS): www.olemiss.edu/mathed/contest/contests.htm

- The MATHMAN (Kindergarten and up): www.shout.net/~mathman

- Math Mastery (Elementary and Middle School): www.mathmastery.com

- Maths Year 2000 (Preschool–HS): www.mathsyear2000.org

- Math Word Problems for Children (Elementary and Middle School) www.mathstories.com

- MathsNet: Mathematics in Education (puzzles, games, books, software, etc. for all ages–UK): www.MathsNet.net

- Mega Mathematics (Middle School and HS): www.c3.lanl.gov/mega-math/index.html

- Millennium Mathematics Project: Bringing Mathematics to Life (Cambridge, UK): www.mmp.maths.org.uk/index.html

- National Council of Teachers of Mathematics Family Corner (K–12): www.nctm.org/corners/family/index.htm

- NRICH Math, Univ. of Cambridge, UK (Elementary–HS): www.nrich.maths.org.uk

- National Security Agency Kids Page (Elementary–HS): www.nsa.gov/programs/kids

- PBS Kids Cyberchase: pbskids.org/cyberchase

- Pentomino Puzzle (Elementary–HS): www.theory.csc.uvic.ca/~cos/inf/misc/PentInfo.html

- Problems to Enjoy (Middle grades–Grades 7–9, UK): www.1000problems.com

- Rich Problem-Solving Contexts (esp. geometry projects): www.math.okstate.edu/~rpsc

- Shack's Math Problems (Middle School–HS): www.thewizardofodds.com/math

- Word Problems for Kids (Grades 5–12): www.stfx.ca/special/mathproblems/welcome.html

Math and Science Competitions

For children who enjoy mathematics competitions, the following sites include competitions around the world. Some require school or teacher sponsorship and others may be entered independently.

- American Mathematics Competitions (Middle School and HS): www.unl.edu/amc

- American Regions Mathematics League (HS): www.arml.org

- American Statistical Association Poster and Project Competitions (K–12): www.amstat.org/education/poster1.html

- Casio Calculator Problem Solving Contests (Elementary–HS): www.casio.com/education/index.cfm?page=/education/contests.htm

- Craftsman/NSTA Young Inventors Awards Program (Grades 2–8): www.nsta.org/programs/craftsman

- First LEGO League (FLL) Jr. Robotics Competition (ages 9–14): www.firstlegoleague.org

- FIRST Robotics Competition (HS): www.usfirst.org

- High School Mathematical Contest in Modeling (HiMCM): www.comap.com/highschool/contests/himcm/index.html

- Intel Science Talent Search (HS): www.intel.com/education/sts/index.htm

- Junior Science and Humanities Symposium (HS): www.jshs.org

- Let's Get Real Team Academic Competitions (Grades 6–12): www.LGReal.org

- The Mandelbrot Competition (HS): www.mandelbrot.org

- MATHCOUNTS, National Society of Professional Engineers Information Center (Middle Grades math competition): www.mathcounts.org

- Math League (HS): www.mathleague.com

- Mathematical Olympiads for Elementary and Middle Schools: www.moems.org

- Mathematics Pentathlon (Game Competition for K–7th grade): www.mathpentath.org

- Millennium Prize Problems (College and up): claymath.org/prizeproblems/index.htm

- NASA Student Involvement Program (K–12): www.nsip.net/

- National Engineering Aptitude Search (NEAS+), Tests of Engineering Aptitude, Mathematics, and Science (TEAMS), National Engineering Design Challenge (NEDC), Junior Engineering Technical Society (Middle School and HS): www.jets.org

- National Engineers Week Future City Competition (K–12): www.eweek.org

- Odyssey of the Mind (K–College): www.odysseyofthemind.com

- Science Olympiad (Elementary–HS): www.soinc.org
- Solve It! Middle Grades Math Problem Solving Program: www.udel.edu/educ/solveit
- South African Mathematics Olympiad: ridcully.up.ac.za/samo
- Stock Market Game Worldwide (Grades 4–College): www.smgww.org
- ThinkQuest (Primary-HS): www.thinkquest.org
- Toshiba/NSTA ExploraVision Awards (K–12): www.toshiba.com/tai/exploravision
- USA Computing Olympiad (HS): usaco.uwp.edu
- USA Mathematical Talent Search (Middle School and HS): www.nsa.gov/programs/mepp/usamts.html

Summer and School Year Opportunities for Precollege Students

The following include a few of the opportunities for summer and school year mathematics programs for strong students. Most of these are for high school students.

- AMS Listing of Summer Math Camps and Programs for High School Students: www.ams.org/employment/mathcamps.html
- The Arnold Ross Summer Program at Ohio State (HS): www.math.ohio-state.edu/ross
- Building Dreams Through Engineering: Summer Camp for Middle School Girls, University of Illinois at Urbana-Champaign: www.wie.uiuc.edu/games
- Boston's University's Program in Mathematics for Young Scientists PROMYS (HS): math.bu.edu/people/promys
- Canada/USA MathCamps (HS): www.mathcamp.org
- Center for Talented Youth at Johns Hopkins University (Elementary–HS): www.jhu.edu/gifted
- Clay Mathematics Institute (HS): claymath.org/students/index.htm
- The Duke University TIP programs (Middle School): www.tip.duke.edu
- Gifted Math Program at the University at Buffalo (academic year): wings.buffalo.edfu/org/giftedmath
- The Johns Hopkins CTY and SET programs (K–12): www.jhu.edu/~gifted

- Math Forum Listing of High School Math Camps & Summer Programs: mathforum.org/students/high/opps.html

- The Northwestern University Center for Talent Development (Preschool–HS): www.ctd.northwestern.edu

References

Jensen, Linda R. (August 1980). Developing mathematical creativity. Presentation at the International Congress on Mathematical Education (ICME), Berkeley, California.

Lobel, Arnold. (1979). *Frog and Toad are friends.* New York: Harper Collins.

National Council of Teachers of Mathematics. (1980). *An agenda for action: Recommendations for school mathematics of the 1980s.* Reston, VA: Author.

National Council of Teachers of Mathematics. (2000). *Principles and standards for school mathematics.* Reston, VA: Author.

Schmidt, William H., McKnight, Curtis C., and Raizen, A. (1996). *Splintered vision: An investigation of U.S. mathematics and science education.* Washington, DC: U. S. National Research Center.

Sheffield, Linda J. (Ed.). (1999). *Developing mathematically promising students.* Reston, VA: National Council of Teachers of Mathematics.

Sheffield, Linda J. (February 2000). Creating and developing promising young mathematicians. *Teaching Children Mathematics, 6*(6), 416–419, 426.

Sheffield, Linda J. (Fall 2000). Characteristics of mathematically promising students. *KAGE Update: The Newsletter of the Kentucky Association for Gifted Education,* pp. 7–8.

Sheffield, Linda J., Bennett, Jennie, Berriozábal, Manuel, DeArmond, Margaret, & Wertheimer, Richard. (December 1995). *Report of the Task Force on the Mathematically Promising.* (NCTM News Bulletin, vol. 32. Reston, VA: National Council of Teachers of Mathematics.

Sheffield, Linda Jensen, & Cruikshank, Douglas E. (2000). *Teaching and learning elementary and middle school mathematics* (4th ed., updated). New York: John Wiley

Sheffield, Linda Jensen, Findell, Carol R., Gavin, M. Katherine, & Greenes, Carole E. (2000). *Awesome math problems for creative thinking.* Chicago: Creative Publications.

Tompert, Ann. (1997). *Grandfather Tang's story.* Cleveland Heights, OH: Dragonfly Books.

Index